Photo by Marc Wolens

About the Author

This is Rick Carson's fourth book for HarperCollins. His seminal work, *Taming Your Gremlin®*, has had a remarkable track record. Translated into several languages, *Taming Your Gremlin* has been a consistent seller since 1984. For thousands in a cross-section of cultures and circumstances, the Gremlin-Taming Method serves as a foundation for responding to everyday challenges and for living a satisfying life.

For over thirty-five years Rick has been a counselor, personal and executive coach, and trainer for mental health professionals, businesses, and nonprofit organizations. His work is used in the training of psychotherapists, personal and executive coaches, substance abuse specialists, corrections personnel, teachers, corporate executives, clergy, and others. He is a former faculty member at the University of Texas Southwestern Medical School and a clinical member and approved supervisor for the American Association for Marriage and Family Therapy.

Rick is the founder of the Gremlin Taming Institute in Dallas, Texas. For more information: www.tamingyourgremlin.com.

A Master Class in
gremlin-Taming®

☆ ☆ ☆ ☆
        ☆

A Master Class in Gremlin-Taming®

⭐ ☆ ☆ ☆ ☆

The Absolutely Indispensable Next Step
for Freeing Yourself from the
Monster of the Mind

Rick Carson

Collins

An Imprint of HarperCollinsPublishers

HarperCollins books may be purchased for educational, business, or sales promotional use. For information, please write: Special Markets Department, HarperCollins Publishers, 10 East 53rd Street, New York, NY 10022.

FIRST EDITION

Designed by Nancy B. Field

Illustrations by Novle Rogers

Printed on acid-free paper

Library of Congress Cataloging-in-Publication Data

Carson, Richard David.
    A master class in gremlin-taming : the absolutely indispensable next step for freeing yourself from the monster of the mind / Rick Carson. — 1st Collins paperback ed.
            p. cm.
    Includes bibliographical references and index.
        ISBN 978-0-06-114840-8
1. Happiness. 2. Success — Psychological aspects. 3. Self-perception. 4. Choice (Psychology) I. Title.

BF575.H27C377 2008
158.1 —dc22

                                        2007032028

08   09   10   11   ❖/RRD   10   9   8   7   6   5   4   3   2   1

To my friend
Nancy Ferguson
and
in loving memory of
my brother Frank

Contents

Acknowledgments

I suppose I've already acknowledged Nancy Ferguson by dedicating this book to her, and I'm certain she's thinking as she reads this, "Okay, enough already." But there's more. If there were a contest for best friend, Nancy would win it. She does "friend" the best—not just in relation to me but to everybody (dogs and cats included). I value enormously Nancy's loyalty, her clearheaded forthrightness, and her support of my work. Our association helped make this book better and writing it a more enjoyable process.

Jane Massengill, the director of the Gremlin-Taming Institute, has been a true gift in my life. To have a person of Jane's wisdom and talent embrace my work is, to say the least, gratifying. I'm deeply indebted to Jane for her encouragement and hard work. Her enthusiasm about gremlin-taming has inspired me to preserve quality at all costs. Jane has my blessing to put her own spin on gremlin-taming, blend it with her own ideas, and come out with whatever she wants. I trust her completely.

To my two favorite sidekicks—my loving wife, Leti, and our son, Jonah—your love, friendship, and enthusiasm about what I have to offer mean everything to me. Thanks for knowing me so well and hanging with me anyway.

To Novle Rogers, whose art embellishes all of my books, I'd like to offer a West Texas buddy-to-buddy sock on the arm. Reconnecting with Novle to produce this book has been a delight.

Watching Novle work is thrilling, and having him as my compadre makes me happy as a hoot owl. I'm grateful as can be.

Working with Toni Sciarra, my editor at HarperCollins, has been a privilege and a pleasure. Toni and I also worked together on the revised edition of *Taming Your Gremlin*. She understands not only my message but the challenge of presenting it in a way that is entertaining and practical. This book is better because of Toni's input. I couldn't ask for a better teammate.

Many thanks, too, to my agent, Al Zuckerman, at Writers House, for encouraging this project and seeing it through. I'm honored to be a part of Al's stable and to have a man of his stature behind me.

Doug Rucker, whose interview with me appears within, is one of the most talented people I know. I greatly admire Doug and his work as a creative marketing professional. Doug's sense of "what works" is almost spooky—and he speaks his mind. His friendship, his feedback, and his genuine interest in my work have been priceless.

My friend Kathy Ross is an artist with a discriminating eye and impeccable good taste. She's quite familiar with my work and a straight shooter. So when I sought feedback on the manuscript, Kathy was among the few I asked to read it. Her input was right on, and her timely enthusiastic support meant a great deal to me.

My assistant, Kim Harrison, was new on the job when I signed the contract for this book. Little did she know what she was getting into. She's kept the office fires burning, freeing me up to scratch my head and stare at blank paper. Kim's friendship, good humor, and hard work have made even the weird days enjoyable.

And most important, my heartfelt appreciation to Prem Rawat, lovingly known by many, including myself, as Maharaji. Thank you, Maharaji, for directing me to the true love within me and for your continual reminders to trust my heart.

Introduction:

★ ☆ ☆ ☆ ☆

Before You Begin This Book

When my publisher approached me about writing a book with a suggested working title of *A Master Class in Gremlin-Taming*, I was elated yet reluctant. Over the twenty-five-plus years since *Taming Your Gremlin*® was first published, I've had an abundant flow of requests for such a work, and certainly during that time I've guided thousands in using the Gremlin-Taming Method to go deeper and learn more. But writing a new book presented a special challenge. Here's how.

The Gremlin-Taming Method is tried and true and complete. Nothing is missing in the description of the method as it appears in the original work. The clarity, simplicity, and, most important, the practicality of *Taming Your Gremlin* is, I think, what accounts for its mass appeal and what I appreciate the most about it.

So how could I take you to a deeper level without gumming up the works and complicating what is an elegantly simple process, if I do say so myself? The answer now seems obvious. I'll do so the same way I've done for over thirty-five years, with thousands of seekers like you and me, many of whom are themselves professional inner guides and more than a little familiar with gremlin-taming. Some have read the book many times and have attended numerous workshops and training sessions with me. I'll do with you precisely what I do with them: wing it. But it will be methodical winging, composed of targeted responses to the most common queries and inquiries regarding gremlin-taming.

In the interest of providing you the most personally meaningful experience of gremlin-taming possible, my valued colleague and the director of the Gremlin Taming Institute, Jane Massengill, and I have elicited the help of thousands of practitioners of the Gremlin-Taming Method. Jane and I have reviewed audio excerpts of media interviews, reviewed questions from readers as well as from current and former students, scratched our heads, and gnashed our teeth in an attempt to grab the most commonly asked questions regarding gremlin-taming.

Every few months for the past five years, we have held "Ask the Gremlin-Tamer" teleclasses. We've reviewed these as well. In addition, we sent an e-mail through the Gremlin Taming Institute, to let people know that the book you now hold was forthcoming and to invite questions. While this is not to be a book of "frequently asked questions," much of what follows will be a composite of my responses to the most common queries and inquiries.

And we're going to cover new territory. Several years ago I asked myself a simple question: What did I have to do to make certain I gave my clients my best shot? The answer came quickly: In the time I'm with them, devote every ounce of my being to them. A seven-word acronym blossomed into my consciousness. The acronym is I CREATE. The values and behaviors encompassed in I CREATE have become treasures to me. I've applied them far beyond my relationships with my clients.

In fact, I make every effort to lead my life, breath to breath, in accordance with them. Doing so has enhanced my life. I've also shared I CREATE with private clients, with trainees, in workshops, and with friends, and for many the seven keys it contains have become guideposts for maximizing the richness of experience inherent in every moment.

The acronym I CREATE holds within it the Seven Keys for Creating Rewarding Relationships. Not just with people, but with all and everything.

Gremlins are as unique as the souls on which they labor. Yours is no exception. My hope is that what follows will make the gremlin-taming process as clear and applicable to your unique inner life as possible. So, I've made every effort to use personal experiences and real-life vignettes to clarify, illuminate, and dramatize gremlin-taming in action. I think you will find the content accessible, practical, and immediately applicable. This book looks more closely than the original at how to actually apply the Gremlin-Taming Method day in and day out. I hope it inspires you to begin doing so immediately.

If you are one of the half dozen or so people who read my second book, *Never Get a Tattoo* (HarperCollins 1990), you may recognize a few vignettes. I included them, often with slight modifications, to drive home and clarify key points—and because I think you will like them.

I also review many of the key principles of gremlin-taming, so it's not essential to read *Taming Your Gremlin* before you read this book. If, however, you have not read *Taming Your Gremlin*, and you find as you read on that you want to deepen your understanding, I strongly suggest that you get yourself a copy. It's been a consistent seller for about twenty-five years, and readers in a cross-section of cultures and circumstances have let me know that they value, more than a little, the theoretical underpinnings contained in their tattered, underlined, and highlighted copies.

Because of the large type, the illustrations, the gremlin

metaphor itself, and the fact that you've probably found this book in a self-help section, the material it contains may seem simplistic. It isn't. It is simple, but it is not simplistic—or easy to integrate. In fact, that is precisely the reason for the look and style of the book. So I'd like to offer a tip that you might find helpful. If I were you (and of course I'm not), I'd read no more than fifteen minutes at a sitting. Small bites are easier to digest. Having said this, I certainly don't want to get off on the wrong foot in our relationship by being patronizing. My concern is no doubt tainted with projection born of the skimpy nature of my own attention span. You know you and your learning style. I don't. The "fifteen-minute suggestion" is just that—a suggestion.

So you're about to get information. A lot of it. But there is a difference between information and knowledge. The latter results only from direct experience. My fervent hope is that the information that follows will be a stepping-stone on your path to the knowledge of who you really are and of the beautiful experience that lies within you.

A Master Class in Gremlin-Taming®

Chapter 1

The Bottom Line

Bundles of shingles and buckets of tar grow heavy quickly, and while the boxcars we spent hour after hour loading offered some shade, they blocked any hope of a breeze. Summer was half over, and I was glad I'd return to Texas Tech in the fall. For Jim Turnbow and the other dock men, there would likely be no reprieve.

Jim Turnbow had been to prison twice for assault, and every man on the dock knew it. He was forty-five plus and tall, with shiny, wavy black hair. He had a wind-worn face, long sinewy muscles that reminded me of steel cables, and a body swirled with tattoos, including one of a panther on his right forearm. He moved with an undaunted sureness, which I found intimidating. I never saw Jim smile, and he rarely spoke.

Jim and I and the rest of the men on the loading dock got a twenty-five-minute lunch break every day. Though the West Texas wind blew hot and dusty, we ate outside on the dock to escape the smell of burning tar inside the factory.

One day, as I sat on the dock practically merging with my baloney sandwich, I sensed Jim's eyes on me. I risked a glance

1

at him. He was squatting directly across from me, eating a turnip with his pocketknife. His dark eyes were locked in on me. I felt small and brand spanking new, and I tried to grin. My face wouldn't cooperate, and I felt my lip twitching. Then, in a crisp, quick tone, Jim spat out, "Rick!" His cold black eyes pointed right at mine.

My heart skipped a beat, and my soul snapped to attention. Until then, Jim had spoken to me only rarely and briefly, and he had never called me by name.

Jim gestured with his knife as he spoke, his thumb pressing a slice of turnip against the flat side of the blade.

"When you're dead . . ." He leaned toward me, his already level gaze became a piercing glare, and his hand, the knife, and the turnip slice began quivering with the crazed conviction of a man being thunderstruck by the truth. Wide-eyed, I gulped.

"When you're dead . . ." he repeated with greater force, his eyes glazed and wilder now.

"When you're dead . . ." he said again, through clenched teeth this time, and louder, "you're a dead peckerhead." Then he got up and walked back into the factory.

Chapter 2

Birth and Death

Jim had a point. Life as we know it has a definite beginning and a definite end. I know. I was there, not only at my own birth but at the birth of my son, Jonah. I'm fond of saying I delivered him. It's a lie, but I'm fond of saying it. I was there, and the birth did occur in our bedroom, and I did sort of receive him and cut the cord and all—but deliver him? No way.

I expected the whole event to be, you know, eventful. A Gregorian chant upon his arrival would not have surprised me. But there was no Gregorian chant. I just sort of looked down, and there in my hands was a small, living human, looking like a cross between Alfred E. Neuman and a Smurf. But I was there, so I know there is birth.

And I've witnessed death, too. More times than I'd like to recall. When life leaves a body, it's obvious to everybody present. It modifies relationships. It won't be long after your life leaves your body that even your lovers and loyal friends won't choose to hang with you.

So there is birth and there is death. Between them is a steady stream of precious moments known as your existence.

Eventually, it will be represented by a dash between two dates. In actuality, it is a series of breaths, each holding within it an opportunity to fully experience your life, or to dampen it, to ignore it, or even to extinguish it.

Staying aware of and responding gracefully to this choice, breath to breath, is the key to a richly satisfying existence.

Enjoying your life is a breath-to-breath activity.

Chapter 3

One Breath at a Time

Breaths come one at a time. You can't take the next one until you take the current one.

I value my breaths. They've been coming in and going out since I arrived on the planet, and more often than not, I must admit, I take them for granted. Other times, I'm filled with appreciation for each and every one. I've no idea when they'll stop coming—how large the cache is—so I'm hesitant to squander any by stumbling through precious moments in a half sleep, or, worse yet, devoting many breaths' worth of time to unworthy endeavors or displeasing encounters.

My *intention*, in any given moment, is to pay *attention*. Call it being aware, being mindful, or simply being awake during my waking hours. I'm certainly no master of the process, but I am a sincere student most days. My mind, however, has a different idea. My mind, as my friend Jimmie Dale Gilmore sings, has a mind of its own.

Chapter 4

The Mind Is a Terrible Thing

Direct experience has its own language, and it's not the language of the mind. The mind is not interested in knowing, just in knowing about. Your mind is a giant warehouse filled with remnants and representations of direct experience: snapshots, beliefs (opinions to which you've developed loyalty), assumptions, concepts, memories, wild ideas, and foregone conclusions. In the warehouse, hoping you'll stop by, is a monster—the monster of the mind. Sometimes he'll do his best to convince you to visit. Other times, you drop in of your own accord—to remember, fantasize, analyze, scrutinize, plan, problem solve, or simply meander up and down the aisles. The warehouse is gigantic, so sometimes when you drop by, you and the monster don't cross paths.

But when you and he do encounter each other, he will use what is stored in the mind to divert you from the direct experience of your very own life as it is unfolding for you right here and right now. He'll also use what's stored in your mind to create painful regrets, horrifying fears, lofty expectations, unrealistic hopes, dread, self-doubt, deep resentment, hubris, and humiliation, all suited to your unique vulnerabilities.

Could it be we've had our semantics backwards all this time? Maybe "losing your mind" is a good thing? Is being "mindless" more enlivening than being "mindful"? Is it any wonder we sometimes want to give people a "piece of our mind," usually because they've disrupted our "peace of mind"?

Okay, maybe the mind is not all bad. It just needs to be managed, like a bank account. Sure, it can be a pit of dread. But it's a glory-hole of possibilities, too. The meanderings of your mind include fantasy, memory, lovely notions, and half-baked ideas. Within your mind you make up how it is and decide how it will be. Within your mind you bring in hope and conjure up torment. You score coups and create the blues.

Within your mind you can tune in an infinite number of channels, including the Drama channel, the Romance channel, the Horror channel, the Sex channel, the You Are the Top of the Heap channel, the Problem-Solving channel, and the What-Ifs and the If Onlys channels. Within your mind you can be king of the hill and scum of the earth.

Your mind contains beautiful scenes of expansive mountain ranges and fields of fresh daisies. But it definitely has some unsavory areas. It's got dark, dank, corners wherein dwells the villain that is the source of all that's not right with you, me, and the world. He's your gremlin, the monster of your mind. And when he's dominating the scene, there is no doubt about it—the mind is a terrible thing.

Chapter 5

True Love and Your Heart of Hearts

You're not your mind (though you'd be a bore without it), and you're not your gremlin. Because you're alive, you're fortunate enough to have within you an infinite, sustaining force that keeps your heart pumping, your lungs expanding, and more. That sustaining force has come together with your finite body to create the entity that answers to your name.

The two are connected by your breath. While the sustaining power within you can't be captured by a word, it's had a slew of them assigned to it. In our time together, let's you and I call that life force "true love." Here's an adapted version of how I described true love in the revised edition of *Taming Your Gremlin*.

TRUE LOVE

No description of the experience of true love can do justice to its glory. True love is both subtly and powerfully perfect. True love is not a thought (though certainly you can have loving thoughts). True love is an experience. True love is trustworthy. Just as the sun is always shining whether you can see it or not, true love exists within you always, whether or not you are attentive to it.

When true love comes into your awareness, it permeates your experience, and you feel content, peaceful, and satisfied.

The experience of true love is always available, though I'll be the first to admit, it is easier to tap into and enjoy under some circumstances more than others. Getting a sliver of light between you and your gremlin certainly helps.

Experiencing true love does not require something or someone to love—though you may feel true love inside yourself in the presence of certain people and things. Nor do you insure yourself a large dose of true love by smiling a lot, talking softly, or hugging people with whom you'd rather just shake hands.

The experience of true love differs from the experience of excitement, sexual feeling, adoration, or desire, though these pleasurable sensations increase in lip-smacking intensity when laced with, or founded upon, true love. Pleasurable stimulation can be thrilling—ask your taste buds or your genitals—but even a first-class titillating tingle remains only pleasurable stimulation until you are awakened to the experience of true love lying in a half sleep within your heart of hearts.

YOUR HEART OF HEARTS

Your heart of hearts is the home of true love and thus of simple peace, contentment, and satisfaction. X-ray, even dissection, will not reveal your heart of hearts. Your heart of hearts is not your physical heart, though it is located behind your breastbone. Its breadth and perimeter vary moment to moment, even breath to breath. Awareness of your heart of hearts may be easier for you to experience at some times than at others. You can't be in two places at once, so if you're lost in the world of mind or engaging with your gremlin, you'll likely be out of touch with your heart of hearts.

By the same token, as you become better at taming your gremlin and practicing the I CREATE method I'll introduce to you shortly, you'll find that tapping into and trusting your heart of hearts will come more easily. You may eventually find that your primary way of *feeling* your existence is through your heart of hearts and the true love that is its essence. Your heart of hearts may well become the primary determinant of what pleases you, and you, in turn, may well begin to select actions that please it. Consciously or unconsciously, you may already do so.

From this point forward, when referring to your heart of hearts, I will simply use the word "Heart" and capitalize it.

As you learn to tame your gremlin and to tap into and enjoy your experience of your Heart, you are going to become increasingly able to detect what configurations of props and players make it easier for you to tap into the true love within it. With your gremlin out of the way, your Heart will guide you toward experiences that stimulate true love and away from experiences that don't. The true love within you can help you select whom to hang out with, what props and players to surround yourself with, and what activities to engage in.

True love is the natural state of your Heart. True love is not something you have to create or build. True love is the core of your being. True love is the essence of who you really are. True love is rich beyond your wildest dreams and most loving notions. True love can't be described, only hinted at by words and phrases like "perfect," "just right," "natural," and even "true love." It is in you right this moment. It's behind your breath. It's yours. It's a gift.

And you don't have to be religious, a swami, an avatar, or well heeled in order to experience it. It's humming away inside of you at this moment, and you would be more able to tap into it and enjoy it if it weren't for a vile, ill-intentioned bully with whom you must contend—a pest—who, like your Heart, exists within you. He is the monster of the mind we discussed earlier, and he is hell-bent on diverting you from the true love and simple peace lying in a half sleep within your Heart, and from maximizing the richness of each moment of your existence. That's right: vile and vicious.

Chapter 6

Your gremlin

Your gremlin is the macabre master of misery lurking in the shadows of your very own mind. Your gremlin is not your negative thoughts and traumatic past experiences. He's not your fears, regrets, or self-limiting concepts. He's the one who uses them—and more—to create elaborate cinematic works suited to your unique vulnerabilities. And he's the one who seduces you into watching them and into confusing them with the pure experience of your breath-to-breath existence.

Your gremlin is your gremlin by virtue of his intention, and his intention is to make you miserable by consistently diverting your attention from the simple peace and contentment already within your Heart. Untamed, he will destroy your health, foul up your relationships, dampen your creativity, hamper your productivity, send you tumbling into low-down funks, and wind you up into fits of panic.

As I emphatically stated in the revised edition of *Taming Your Gremlin*, gremlin-taming has nothing to do with a Tom and Jerry cartoon in which one sees Tom or Jerry with an angel on one shoulder and a devil and/or gremlin on the other.

Gremlin-taming is about freeing yourself from that entire dialogue.

Where does your gremlin come from? I don't know. But
he's with you now, and he will continue to be with you so long
as you are on the planet. He's a thief, out to steal your attention moment to moment, breath to breath. Your gremlin is not
cute.

Your gremlin is probably at this very moment beginning to
go wild. After all, his sole purpose is to divert you from finding the simple peace inside of you, and his (or her) job is a lot
easier when he can hide outside of your awareness. He hates
that I'm exposing him. Hear his chatter, but don't take it too
seriously. He may say something like this:

"You already know what this guy has to say. Why read on? Close the book."

or

"You have more important things to do. Time's a-wasting! Close the book."

or

"Life isn't a bowl of cherries. Settle for what you have. Close the book."

Your gremlin is tricky. Of course, he'll try using his obvious weapons like fear, intimidation, put-downs, resentments, and regrets, but his arsenal is far more sophisticated than you might imagine. Several years back, I got some good advice. It's helpful when you are confronted by a particularly powerful gremlin tactic.

Chapter 7

Good Advice

Still sweaty and stiff from our racquetball game, Harry and I sat outside my house in his shiny new Mercedes. That morning's skirmish for the top of the athletic heap had been especially intense—the consummate competitive encounter, demanding of each combatant a honed mind and a toned body. The court was our battlefield. We were men. Real men, just like in the television commercials—skin glistening with perspiration, headbands, Nikes—only shorter and balder and a little older, maybe. But what the hell, we were males—the hairy sex—virile, courageous, congenial, intellectual—brethren (albeit in the broadest sense), or distant cousins, maybe, of the big names: Abraham. Isaac. Elvis.

Harry had beaten me two out of three games. In the locker room I'd belted out "Good game!" and given him a swat on the back. It was a confident "Who cares? It's only a game; it's the exercise that counts" kind of swat. I had adorned it with a casual whistle—"Old Man River," I think, or "Teddy Bears' Picnic." I caught a glimpse of myself in the mirror, a strained smile hardly masking the fire flashing in my eyes. There I was, whistling and swatting, all the while having rapid-fire fantasies of bashing Harry's face in with my racquet—the side of the racquet, the hard part. How could I be such a phony? It was easy. I hate to lose. At times like these I covet my right to be petty and small. I wasn't about to crawl out of my rat hole—not yet. I gotta be me.

The five-minute ride to my house was quiet but for my whistling. Harry's shiny new Mercedes was parked at my curb. There we sat: me brooding, Harry gloating.

We lit up a couple of hand-wrapped Macanudos. It was a ritual we had repeated almost weekly for years. The game, the ride, the cigar, the sweat, and the swat. But this morning was unique. Not just because Harry outscored me, but because it was the morning of my fiftieth birthday. My fiftieth birthday, and he had mopped the court with me. My fiftieth birthday, and he was styling the shiny new ride. Here we were, straddling the seesaw of life, his head getting warmed by the sun, and me so weighted down with a wet cloak of the beady-eyed, tiny-mouthed, touch-me-I'll-bite blues that I could barely see any light at all. Worse yet, Harry had turned fifty a month earlier and had thirty full days' worth of life experience on me.

There we sat, the green kid cowering in the shadow of the confident old pro. I wanted to bite a chunk out of his leg. I wanted to bring him to his knees. I wanted him down in the junkyard with me. But I played it cool. I stopped whistling long enough to stretch real big and faked a casual "La-di-da, life's just a bowl of cherries" yawn. I ended the yawn with "So . . ." as in "So, it's been swell . . ."

I opened the car door and had one foot on the ground when I heard Harry ask, "So what?" Seemingly innocent verbiage, I know, but I wasn't fooled for a minute. Subtle though it was, I spotted the self-glorifying weasel's veiled arrogance.

It was just like in racquetball. The momentum was on Harry's side of the car. His confidence was up. Mine was down. He felt big and proud. I felt shriveled up and mean.

I waited for an opening, and then I hurled the gauntlet: "So, big fella, you're older and wiser. Lay some wisdom on me. Give me some advice on turning fifty."

I felt it. The "best man" momentum shifted slightly to my side of the car. The gauntlet was on Harry's side. He paused. His upper lip twitched slightly. He wanted to stay smooth, but I'd broken his stride with my deft delivery. Pumped with the confidence of his win, Harry snatched up that gauntlet, leaned back in his broad Mercedes seat, took a pull on that big see-gar, and let go of a smoke ring that would have made the Great Gildersleeve green with envy. It was his day. The momentum was again in his favor. My mouth got dry. I braced myself. Then he looked at me, steely-eyed, and with the unflinching confidence of the Lone Ranger, he laid it on me. "Never get a tattoo," he said.

The words went straight to my heart. I'm no Spinoza, but I knows the truth when I hears it. I blew a pretty fair smoke ring of my own and nodded thanks.

I'm a solid sixty-three now. I've not gotten a tattoo, and my life since that morning over thirteen years ago has been upwards of fine and dandy. I believe in sharing a good thing, so I'm passing Harry's tidbit of universal wisdom on to you. It's sound advice. It says something about the trap of having permanently inscribed on your arm, your hip, or your psyche, for that matter, a concept of who you are or who you imagine you're supposed to be—something about being careful about what you advertise, and something about the myth of unalterable truths.

Your gremlin is a superb tattoo artist and a hypnotist as well. Since shortly after you arrived on the planet, he's been whispering in your ear hypnotic messages about who you are and how the world works. These hypnotic messages are tattoos on your psyche. Your gremlin adores these Hypnotic Pre-Convictions because they dampen the freshness of your moment-to-moment experience.

Chapter 8

Your Heart,
the Natural You,
Your Hypnotic
Pre-Convictions, and
Your Advertising

Your Heart is the home and source of true love and simple contentment. It is the essence of the Natural You, the one who learned to walk and talk—the experiencer and observer of all you experience and observe.

THE WHOLE PERSON DIAGRAM

Let's let this symbol represent your Heart, and the love that is the essence of who you really are.

And let this heart with a ring around it represent the Natural You.

Wrapped around the Natural You is a layer of beliefs you have *about* who you are—your psychic tattoos. These concepts about yourself and the world are quite prominent in your day-to-day experience. After all, from the time you were pushed out onto the planet, finding yourself smack dab in the middle of whatever unique drama you happened to slide out into, you have been bombarded with experiences. From these experiences you've formed all sorts of ideas about who you are, who you imagine you're supposed to be, and how the world works.

You have ideas about how lovable you are, how likable you are, how smart you are, how creative you are, how your relationships will unfold, how successful you will be, and even how you stack up in relation to your peers. These concepts, or Hypnotic Pre-Convictions (HPCs), are wrapped tightly around the natural you.

You've acquired your Hypnotic Pre-Convictions from how others have responded to you, from what others have told you about yourself, and from your own trials and errors as you have experimented with one action after another. This ring around the Natural You represents these Hypnotic Pre-Convictions.

Given the pervasiveness of the experiences through which you have acquired your Hypnotic Pre-Convictions about yourself, it's no wonder they are hard to spot. You are, in a sense, "in them," or so it seems. Given this aspect of the human condition, isn't it possible that the boundary between who you really are and who you imagine you are has gotten a little blurred? Well, sure it is. Nonetheless, if you are like the rest of us—and you are, to a large extent—you probably carry with you all sorts of Hypnotic Pre-Convictions about yourself.

It will behoove you to remember that any self-concept is false simply because you are not a concept. Based on your concepts, or Hypnotic Pre-Convictions, you have formed another layer that we will call your Act—your advertising, represented by the outer ring below.

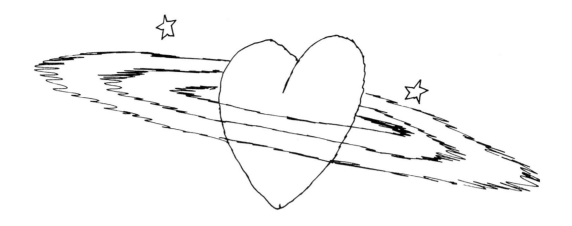

I've met lovable lugs, goody two-shoes, perky princesses, sensitive males, bad girls, beboppers, hunks, metaphysical magi, earth mothers, effervescent evangelists, and more. We start acting early.

When I was ten and my cousin Michael had just turned twelve, we went to see *The Sands of Iwo Jima*, starring John Wayne, at the Plaza Theater in Lubbock, Texas. Michael had plans to meet a girl at the theater. He did. She sat next to him on his left, and I was on his right. He paid more attention to her than to me. He put his arm around her, and every now and then he would turn his head and look at her. This was a clue for her to look at him. She did, every time. And then they'd touch lips—kiss. It looked awkward to me. I understood his motivation. I had kissed a few girls myself in a game of Spin the Bottle a few weeks before this. But where Michael and I were concerned, an uncomfortable shift was occurring. This was, after all, *The Sands of Iwo Jima*, and I thought it would be like when Michael and I saw *Flying Tigers*. We'd be totally enthralled with the movie, and then we'd go home and play like we *were* them—the guys on the big screen. But it didn't work that way.

After the movie, Michael didn't want to play army. He wanted to talk about girls. It felt awkward. Sort of like the awkward kisses between him and her. I remember a disquieting feeling in my body, as if something was ending. I felt suspended and uncomfortable.

Later, at my house, I put on my army helmet, got out my favorite gun (a replica of a German Luger), and went outside and found John and Lester. They were my age and had never kissed girls. We played army. We went to the foxhole we'd been digging for two weeks in a vacant lot. I thought of myself as the John Wayne character. We pretended we were fighting the enemy.

I was standing, holding my Luger, wearing my army helmet, when Jenny Simpson came walking down the sidewalk. She was twelve years old, had taught me how to bebop two weeks earlier, and was one of the girls I had kissed in the Spin the Bottle game. I dove for cover into the foxhole.

We start to develop attachment to our acts early on. Often, we overidentify with them, so when they get confronted, or blown to smithereens, we're not quite sure who we are or how to behave. This is tougher during some stages of life than others. Thus, the infamous "adolescent identity crisis." Being trapped between a view of oneself as a kid and a view of oneself as a bebopping teen is akin to being drawn and quartered. But where inordinate attachment to acts is concerned, no stage of life has exclusive rights.

In one of my stumbling runs at trying to be somebody, I instituted an all-out dress-for-success regimen. It was inspired by my admiration for the natty dress-up style of a former client of mine. At the time, we were both in our mid-forties. He was a distinguished-looking man, well educated, soft spoken, wealthy by his own effort and achievements. In his silk ties, pinstriped suits, and cordovan wingtip oxfords, he was a strik-ing figure. Snazzy, as my dad used to say. In his presence I felt a little shabby, clothes-wise. I decided to dandy up.

At my first opportunity, I pulled from my closet a snappy silk tie. I like ties and buy them on occasion, but I rarely wear them. Probably because when I do, it feels like my first day—as if I'm brand-new. But I pulled out a sharp tie, "the suit" (as my wife, Leti, called it), and a nicely pressed white shirt, put them on, and looked in the mirror. There was no glitz. Something was missing. Then it hit me. Anybody can wear snappy suits, ties, and shirts. The overpowering pizzazz of my client's sharp look clearly emanated from his cordovan wingtip oxfords. I had none. I snatched up Leti and Jonah and dragged them with me to the biggest shoe store in Dallas.

I was a man with a purpose. I was on the hunt for some cordovan wingtip oxfords. Success shoes. Shiny shoes. Daddy shoes. Statement shoes.

In the male shoe world, cordovan wingtip oxfords were top banana. The shoes are still around, but they don't make them the way they used to. The design has changed. Back then, they were big shoes, they were mondo everything, but mostly they were mondo large. Big. And they had wide sledlike soles. They had soles with substance. They trumpeted their wearer's strong character and big bucks. At least they did on my client.

This prince of presence and I had a lot in common—two arms, two legs, and one head. But I fear that is where the similarity ended. He was six feet four inches tall and strikingly handsome. I was and still am five feet eleven inches tall, and,when it comes to looks, I am, in the words of my son, Jonah, then six years old, "about regular." But I found the shoes and bought them and wore them into my office Monday morning.

I was self-conscious. Not whole-body self-conscious, just feet self-conscious. I felt as if God had a spotlight focused on my feet, so all who came within fifteen feet of me would have the opportunity to evaluate the overall effect of my new boppers. There I was—Mister Shoes. They seemed mammoth to me. All I was sure of that day was that I wouldn't topple over. I felt like Ronald McDonald. Not a client or supervisee let me slide. Even the otherwise restrained among them offered at least a side comment—unsolicited, I might add.

"Dress-up day, Rick?"

"Got a big meeting today, Rick?"

One student of mine couldn't resist the opportunity to wink, lightly elbow me in the side, and say, "New earth pads, Big Daddy?" Another otherwise respectful therapist in one of my supervision groups interrupted a case presentation long enough to point at my feet, chortle, and blurt out, "Those feet don't belong to that person."

I still have those cordovan wingtip oxfords. They're in my closet. About once a year I put them on just to see if I fit them yet.

There's nothing wrong with a good act, and you can have a big time getting your act together. You can even get props to go with your act (cars, clothes, house, toy German Lugers) and people to go *along* with your act. But it's important to remember where you end and your act begins. If you get too attached to your act, you will feel bad when you perform poorly or don't win critics' acclaim. You'll be best served by selecting an act that is consistent with the Natural You. And let me remind you once again to relax your pact to keep your act intact.

If you like your Hypnotic Pre-Convictions about yourself, you've probably formed an act that is consistent with them. If you don't like who you think you are, then you have probably formed an act that is counter to those beliefs. Either way is fine. Acts are neither innately good nor innately bad. I even help people get their acts together. It is important, however, to remember that your act is simply your current style of presentation and that the distinction between your Heart and your act is an important one. Your gremlin wants this distinction blurred. Then, when your act gets chipped away at or blown to smithereens, which is inevitable from time to time, you'll feel an inordinate depth of fear and despair.

Unless you remain conscious of the distinction between your Heart and your advertising, you will, in the midst of dissonant circumstances and times of rapid change, scrape to preserve your act with the same ardor with which you would fight for your life—by diving into a foxhole, maybe. (In Chapter 5 of the revised edition of *Taming Your Gremlin* I elaborate on Acts as well as on Acts and Relationships. You may choose to review that chapter.)

Gremlin-taming is a process for beginning to get a sliver of light between

Who you really are

and

Your Hypnotic Pre-Convictions
***About* Who You Are**

Chapter 9

Hypnotic Pre-Convictions About How the World Works

You've got outdated HPCs not only about yourself, but about the world and how it works.

It was 1949 or 1950. I wasn't the kind of kid to stay indoors for any length of time, especially on a Saturday, but my attraction and devotion to Big Jon and Sparkie was wholehearted, to put it mildly.

Big Jon and Sparkie were among my best friends. I knew in my bones we'd be even better pals if we could meet face-to-face. But I had no complaints. Plopping myself down in front of our floor-standing Zenith radio every Saturday morning and tuning them in was satisfying enough. Big Jon and Sparkie had conversations about life, played records, or sometimes just told stories, like those about Captain Jupiter, my hero, and his voyages from planet to planet in his spaceship.

Big Jon was a grown-up, and he talked with a mellow but not sappy voice. He kidded Sparkie a lot. Sparkie had a high voice that sounded like a 45 rpm record being played at 78 rpm, only a little slower, so he was easy to understand.

I could see Big Jon in my mind's eye. He was tall, and a little on the heavy side, with glasses. I could see Sparkie, too. He was about six, like me. He was short, with brown hair, a baseball cap, and probably on most days a slingshot in his back pocket. He was always having some sort of keen adventure with his friends, especially his best pal, Rabbit Ears McKeister. I loved my time with Big Jon and Sparkie, so when I heard they were coming to Lubbock, Texas, my very own neck of the woods, nothing was going to stop me from being there with them.

My mother, sensing the fervor that fueled my devotion, didn't let me entertain one doubt as to whether I'd be in the Lubbock High School auditorium when Big Jon and Sparkie came onstage. And I was. There I sat, one of a hundred or more fidgeting munchkins, sporting toothy grins and wide-eyed anticipation. I craned my neck to see the stage, casting my gaze over what seemed like a sea of heads. I remember being a little taken aback to see a lot of other kids there. I suppose I knew somewhere inside me that it might be that way, but the reality of it made my heart hurt. Suppose Big Jon and Sparkie wanted to say something just to me? Or maybe ask me to stop by after the show for a Delaware Punch? Fat chance, now.

Finally, the lights dimmed. In the seconds before they burst on again, my heart almost beat out of my chest. Then, Whammo! Lights up! There they were, seated onstage before my very eyes. Big Jon, almost just as I had pictured him, tall and friendly looking. A little thinner than I'd expected, but definitely—and miraculously, now that I think about it—a familiar face. But who was that with him? That wasn't Sparkie. The little fella *was* short and had brown hair, and when he belted out "Hiya, kids!" he sounded like Sparkie, but he wasn't Sparkie, I couldn't believe my eyes. What was I seeing? My cerebral circuits were bombarded with rapid-fire fantasies—none good! My eyes and my mind were at war. Eyes, surefire and quick; mind, weighted down with expectations. No contest. The eyes had it. Sparkie was a ventriloquist's dummy. A stinking puppet, for crying out loud! I ached with disappointment. My mind froze. My heart turned to stone. I stayed miffed and confused for a week.

But Saturday morning, just before time for Big Jon and Sparkie, my mind cleared and my heart softened. I mean, didn't Big Jon really deserve some credit for going on with the show, given that Sparkie had stayed home (probably caught up with his pal Rabbit Ears in some wild adventure with space invaders or pirates)? True, Big Jon shouldn't have tried to fool us on this one, leastwise not with some dummy. But Big Jon was a kidder, after all, and as for Sparkie—well, I certainly couldn't blame him for wanting to stay home and play with his friends. If he'd come, he probably would've had a lousy time. I did.

I handled this particular shipwreck of perception fairly deftly, employing a sophisticated maneuver known as denial. But restoring one's equilibrium and regaining clarity is not always so easy.

When's the last time you found yourself blown into bedlam by a swift shift in props, players, or perceived reality? An illness or injury, perhaps. Nature on a rampage. or a business fiasco. Or a loss, maybe—of a loved one, your job, or your self-esteem.

There you were, wrapped in your own ideas about how life's oncoming events would unfold; then whammo! You got it right between the eyes—the victim of insensitivity, lack of understanding, downright villainy, and/or your own rigid tattoo of the mind. Either way, unwanted upheaval is a drag.

But the pangs of upheaval are lessened when we are able to separate the actual event from the mere destruction of our Hypnotic Pre-Convictions of what is so. If you allow your gremlin to blur the boundary between a genuine loss or threat and the mere undoing of an HPC, you will definitely stay off balance (i.e., in a pit of despair or a fit of wild-eyed panic) longer than necessary.

On occasion, life is a gentle breeze, but just as often it blows like a bandit. So, having a system for separating out what's really so from your HPCs and your gremlin's chatter *about* what's so is helpful.

Following is an efficient and effective system for separating fact from fantasy and for restoring your equilibrium after a shake-up. The system uses four key questions: What's so? So what? So what? What now?

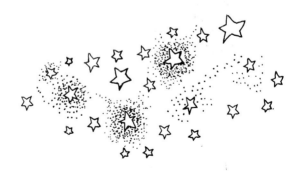

Chapter 10

Four Key Questions

What's So?

The next time you find yourself in the midst of upheaval, ask yourself, "What is the perceived loss?" if any. A friend? A job? Your life? Your self-esteem? What is the perceived threat, if any?

If you look closely at your situation when you next find yourself poised on the brink of panic, you will notice that on the most fundamental level, you fear *abandonment, pain,* or *death.* Your gremlin will pull information from the warehouse of your mind to convince you this is so.

Your job is to assess how real the threat is. Doing so will help you calm yourself. Sorting out reality (what you know for sure) from fantasy (what you imagine) helps. Drag your fear into the light. If you need to gather information in order to distinguish what is real from what you are making up, do so, remembering that it doesn't make good sense to get yourself all worked up over make-believe. Getting worked up for no good reason is precisely what your gremlin wants you to do.

Catastrophic expectations are among the most potent arrows in his quiver. There is no positive cause-and-effect relationship between turning yourself into a nail-biting nervous wreck and taking constructive action.

Assess what has actually been lost or threatened by virtue of whatever critical event has occurred. Separate what you know for sure from what you imagine. Responsible semantics will help. Label an assumption as an assumption. You might want to use phrases such as these:

"I'm assuming that . . ."

or

"I'm imagining that . . ."

or

"I'm making believe that . . ."

or

"I'm scaring the hell out of myself by making up that . . ."

In simple sentences, state what you know for sure. Use accurate language to state the implications you are imagining. For example, "Lulu, my employer, just looked at me with a furrowed brow. I'm *making up* that she's going to give me a bad review." Or, "Several countries that are not real keen on the old US of A right now are acquiring nuclear weapons. *I'm imagining* that we, including me, are going to get blown to bits." Or, "My daughter came in two hours past her curfew last night. I'm scaring myself by *fantasizing* she's pregnant."

Your fantasy may be right on. Who knows? But if you want to restore your equilibrium, it's important to separate what you know for sure from what you imagine. And then ask yourself another important question:

So What?

Get to the immediate imagined consequence, for instance, "I'll lose my job" or "we'll be blown up" or "she's pregnant." And then ask yourself, "So what?" once again.

So What?

Now get to the bottom line. Typically, it will have to do with abandonment, severe pain, or death.

What Now?

Make a logical, sequential, goal-oriented plan composed of small realistic steps. And then take the steps.

Keep in mind that even an abrupt shift in circumstances or perception is a crisis only if you perceive it as a threat, as a loss, or as a threat of a loss.

SO LET'S REVIEW

This is your Heart, the essence of who you really are.

This is the Natural You, including your heart, uncontaminated by HPCs and the mutterings of your mind. The Natural You knows what it knows from pure experience, not from what it has been told.

This is the Natural You surrounded by your Hypnotic Pre-Convictions about who you are.

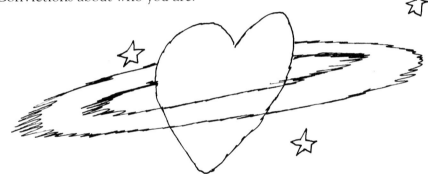

This is the Natural You, including your Heart, surrounded by your Hypnotic Pre-Convictions about who you are, surrounded by your act—your advertising.

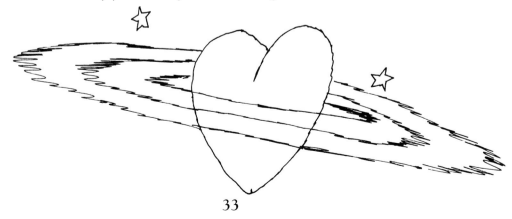

Your Hypnotic Pre-Convictions of the world and how it works constitute a net cast over your pure experience of your very own life.

Each square of the net is an HPC—a concept or belief you hold about the world (and remember: beliefs, even the noblest of them, are just opinions you have developed loyalty to). As you begin to observe the net it will begin to disappear, because a net is, after all, no more than a bunch of holes tied together.

Chapter 11

The Gremlin-Taming Method Revisited

As you begin to observe your Hypnotic Pre-Convictions and your gremlin's chatter you will be in touch with the observer within—the Natural You, the essence of which is your Heart. It's a subtle experience at first. In these moments, a sliver of light is present between who you really are and your ideas about who you are. Beginning to simply notice, to simply feel, if only slightly, the true love that is the essence of who you really are is a delightful experience. It will make you want more.

In more than one media interview, I've been asked to sum up *Taming Your Gremlin*. The truth is, the book is the summary. If I could have made it any simpler or more succinct, I would have. Having said so, I think you will find what follows helpful, whether you are a longtime practitioner of the Gremlin-Taming Method or are just learning about it.

Taken from a recent interview conducted by Doug Rucker of R&D Thinktank in Dallas, these sincere questions and off-the-cuff answers will give you and me solid footing from which we can leap off into the future.

In your presentations and workshops, you say surprisingly little about gremlins. Why?

Because the Gremlin-Taming Method is not really about gremlins—just as a sculpture is not about the stone that ends up on the floor. The Gremlin-Taming Method is a process for moving toward a heightened awareness of who you really are by *simply noticing* and thus evaporating who you are not.

Must we replace negative thinking with positive thinking in order to tame our gremlins?

Positive thinking feels better than negative thinking. Either will affect your present experience and to some extent dictate your future. But your Heart does not need to be positively affirmed. It feels fine. It simply needs to be felt.

You've written that simply noticing is far more powerful than analyzing. Why is simply noticing more effective?

There is a difference between insight and awareness. Insight has to do with figuring out why you are the way you are. Awareness has to do with noticing how you are. On a scale of 0 to 10, an insight is worth about a 3. I don't mean to imply it has no value, because for some people it has great meaning and is very helpful, not to mention interesting.

However, where deep-seated personal growth is concerned, I think of awareness as a 10.

For example, if I said to you, "Can you help me get rid of this pain in my eye?" and you helped me notice that I was jabbing my thumb in my eye, I would probably stop doing so. As in the present moment I noticed and took responsibility for creating the pain by jabbing my very own thumb in my very own eye, I would certainly have a choice as to whether to continue doing so or not. The absurdity in the fact that I was spending precious moments of my life jabbing my thumb in my eye would, in all likelihood, become apparent to me.

But what if I had a Hypnotic Pre-Conviction that I couldn't stop until I figured out *why* I was doing it? And what if I invited you to help me get to the bottom of this horrible eye-jabbing problem? And what if you colluded with me in this misguided investigative endeavor? We could, I suppose, examine the possibility that my father also jabbed his thumb in his eye, or maybe that I came from a long line of eye-jabbers, or perhaps I was a thumb-sucker as a small child and my folks were intolerant of that, so I developed a piss-poor alternative. Or maybe my mother was a super caretaker, a martyr, and I learned from watching her that suffering was noble, and jabbing my thumb in my eye became an easy way to make myself suffer. Absurd as it sounds, this process of "figuring out" is what often happens in professional helper/helpee relationships.

You get the idea. It's simply more efficient to shine a bright light of awareness on outdated beliefs and the behaviors that emerge from them, so that a natural correction can take place, than it is to *try* to *figure out* where those beliefs and behaviors come from. As we begin to really observe our outdated beliefs and behaviors, they often seem absurd in light of our current age and circumstances. Interestingly, even though it is not essential to understand where they come from, when and how we selected them often becomes obvious. Choice is the key here. This is where *simply noticing* comes into play.

Simply noticing is the quintessential skill for quieting the monster of the mind and for beginning to get a sliver of light between the essence of who you really are (your Heart) and your ideas *about* who you are. *Simply noticing* has nothing to do with analyzing the past, predicting the future, or figuring out anything. *Simply noticing* has only to do with *simply noticing*—

paying attention. Your primary tool for *simply noticing* is your awareness.

Your awareness is like a spotlight mounted in the current moment. From its base in the moment called Now, you are directing it. At this moment you are shining it onto my words. You could as easily shine it on what is going on around you or on what is going on within your body. You can even shine your *spotlight of awareness* into the past via your memory, or into the world of make-believe via fantasy. And you can use it to *simply notice* your very own ideas—your concepts about who you are and about how the world works.

Again, concepts are just beliefs, and beliefs, even the noblest of them, are just opinions you've developed loyalty to. We hold them so we can pretend that the world has order and is predictable. This helps us feel safe. Ironically, we sometimes fight to defend our beliefs, creating anything but a safe situation. Some of us defend our self-concepts with the same fervor we would use to defend our lives.

It's important to remember that your self-concept, regardless of how glorious it is, is faulty and confining for one simple reason: You are not a concept.

Someone recently sent me an e-mail saying that for them, "*Simply noticing* is mindfulness in action." "Mindfulness" has come to mean awareness. In that sense, I concur. *Simply noticing* is a tool for making mindfulness a living, moment-to-moment, practical experience. The potency of *simply noticing* as a tool for personal and spiritual evolvement relies in the link between *simply noticing* and what I call the Zen Theory of Change.

What is the Zen Theory of Change?
Simply stated, it is:

I free myself, not by trying to free myself but by *simply noticing* how I am imprisoning myself in the very moment in which I am imprisoning myself.

In other words, freeing yourself doesn't come from trying to bend the bars of the cage and escape. It comes from catching yourself in the act of building the cage.

The process described in the Zen Theory of Change is, of course, universal and, like any truth, existed before the word "Zen" even came into being. Here's how it works:

As you use your awareness to bring an outdated concept or behavior into the light—that is, to *simply notice* it—if it no longer fits for you, it will begin to disappear. You needn't analyze it or fight with it. There is deep within you a powerful force. In the book you now hold, we are calling it true love. It can't really be circled by a word, because it existed before words. This true love is the essence of the Natural You—the observer.

When you were an unsophisticated, funny-looking rookie in this game of life, the Natural You guided you to master complex tasks like walking and talking. Before you knew anything about anatomy or physics, the Natural You noted missteps and corrected them without a conscious thought on your part. As an organism, on the most fundamental level, you would rather be in balance than out of balance. This is the desire of the Natural You, the core of which is your Heart.

Use your power of *simply noticing* to shine a light on your HPCs and on the unproductive Habitual Behavior Patterns (HBPs) that emerge from them. (Unproductive HBPs include such behaviors as jabbing one's thumb in one's eye.) Having *simply noticed* your HPCs and HBPs, the Natural You, guided by your Heart, will take care of the rest. In fact, you can trust the Natural You and your Heart to take from my words what fits for you and to eliminate anything that doesn't.

For goodness' sake, don't get trapped in your mind *trying* to *figure out* anything. Your gremlin's waiting in there to seduce you into spending a lot of time in your mind instead of in your life.

By *simply noticing* your gremlin's chatter and your HPCs as they play through your head, you will become aware of how you are getting in your own way *in the very moment you are getting in your own way.* As you do so you will automatically begin to center and reconnect with the truth of your existence—your Heart. In the moment you *simply notice* an outdated concept, you are in touch, if only subtly, with the noticer, the observer within, the Natural You. It's a *quiet* but very powerful experience.

As you *simply notice* the Natural You, the experience of who you really are will begin to expand. Experience is the key word here. It is not necessary to define or describe who you are. In fact, to do so is to form another concept *about* you, and as I said earlier, any self-concept is limiting and false.

Simply noticing is a skill. It's not a philosophy. It relies on learning to gently control your *spotlight of awareness.* It is the first step in the Gremlin-Taming Method.

The benefits of *simply noticing* as a tool for cleansing the channel between the soul and the persona are inexhaustible.

So, as one begins to simply notice, then what?

Nothing else is required. But you can *play with options* if you want to, and in many instances *playing with options* will speed up the process of deep-seated personal change. I want to emphasize the word "playing" here. *Playing with options* has nothing to do with trying or straining. It has to do with fooling around, experimenting, trying on new possibilities. In *Taming Your Gremlin* I go into great detail about several options with which folks can play, but let's discuss just one here. Let's discuss accenting the obvious.

Fritz Perls, a truly brilliant psychiatrist and teacher, was a genius when it came to accentuating the obvious, and he was one of the several pioneers who developed a potent psychotherapeutic approach known as Gestalt therapy. Often, Fritz would experientially and very vividly accentuate his clients' outdated concepts and the behaviors that emerged from these concepts. As he brought these concepts and behaviors into the light his clients were given the opportunity to observe them with an attitude of "creative indifference." We use this same sort of existential, experiential, phenomenological approach in gremlin-taming.

For example, if you notice yourself shrinking from a conflict with someone or hiding from a challenge, you might try forming a mental picture of yourself acting out your feelings. Imagine yourself growing smaller and smaller, or trembling with fear, or hiding, or cowering in a dark closet. Better yet, if the situation affords you the opportunity, actually scrunch up your posture, or put your head down, or go hide in the closet, or walk as if you have your tail between your legs. This gives the Natural You a chance to observe your strange behavior and the beliefs on which the behavior is based.

Be creative and playful with the process of accentuating the obvious. If, for example, you notice yourself holding in your anger to the point where you feel like a thundercloud, accent the feeling. Hold your breath. Puff up real big, and go look at yourself in the mirror.

And don't overlook one of the simplest ways to accent the obvious, which is to describe to someone what you're noticing about yourself in the very moment you notice it. You might say something like this: "I'm really filled with fury right now, and I feel myself holding it all inside, and I'm puffing up like a thundercloud." Or let's say your gremlin is putting you down, implying that you are incapable or unworthy. Accentuate his chatter by speaking it aloud. Give it a gremlin voice if you want to:

"You miserable lowlife. Your commitment to mediocrity is staggering. You're never gonna amount to anything, but—hey! Think positive. I do. I'm positive you're never gonna amount to anything. And look at ya. You'd have a shot at being attractive if you'd lose a few pounds and get a new head. Give it up. Even those close to you are getting fed up. You're going to end up old and alone, living in an alley and getting gnawed on by rats. Listen, maybe life isn't for everyone."

Even if your gremlin's put-downs and scary taunts have an element of truth in them, as you accentuate your gremlin's chatter you will become quite aware of the absurdity inherent in choosing to spend precious moments of your very own life listening to him. It's really no different from catching yourself in the act of jabbing your very own thumb in your very own eye.

Is there anything else I should simply notice?
Your surroundings, for starters. Notice your surroundings, remembering that your awareness is like a spotlight placed on a pedestal in the current moment. And notice, too, your body—physical sensations, such as points of tension, emotions, your breathing, and your skin.

Your breathing is both a regulator and a barometer of your level of uptightness. In short, when you're feeling free and confident, your breathing is full and clear. You are taking in all the air your body wants and needs, and you are exhaling fully. This is how you breathe when you are feeling good—confident, in the Now, hunky-dory, ginger-peachy. It's how you breathe when you are sleeping soundly and having a nice dream. It's how a yogi or yogini breathes when finally settled into a pose and how a runner breathes when she hits her stride. This sort of breathing entails liberal and lively use of your abdomen—pulling it in when you exhale and releasing it out when you inhale. While this may sound backward to some people, it's how you breathe when you're feeling fine.

The opposite is true when you are uptight. When you create tension you suck in your abdomen as you inhale and force it out as you exhale.

There is an elaborate explication of all this in the revised edition of *Taming Your Gremlin* (pages 32–35). The main thing is to know that your breathing is a barometer and to recognize that when your breathing gets shallow, and you create tension in your body, you are at the front end of making yourself unnecessarily uptight.

Your breath is a regulator in that modifying your breathing—that is, taking in all the air you want and exhaling fully—can greatly reduce your physical manifestation of anxiety.

Is there nothing to be learned from my gremlin's chatter?

Your gremlin is your gremlin by virtue of his intention, not by virtue of the information he whispers in your ear or screams in your face. The information he gives in the midst of his rants is often worth considering. My general view is that almost anything anybody (including my gremlin) says about me has something in it I can learn from. Mutterings such as "You're a screwup and they're going to demote you" or "Better rethink that one, Loser" or "You put your foot in your mouth again, Stupid" may have good information hidden within them. Your gremlin doesn't want his judgment to merely modify your behavior; he wants to defile your entire view of yourself. Maybe you did put your foot in your mouth when you asked when the baby was due, only to discover she wasn't pregnant. A faux pas for sure. We all make them, but that doesn't mean you are a mannerless dirtball.

Feedback in any form is valuable, even if it's from your gremlin. If you can differentiate the information worth considering from your gremlin's abusive muttering and fear tactics, you may learn something. Remember, his intention is to make you miserable. Yours is to increase your capacity for enjoying your life by connecting with your Heart.

To consider information from your gremlin, simply lose the name-calling and negative generalizations about your character and give the information a little thought. I mean it. A *little* thought. A little thought is a lot.

Thinking is oversold. It's not all it's cracked up to be. Sure, it's got its place in small doses, but spending too much time in thought can rain havoc on peace of mind. Five minutes of thought on a given topic is a lot. More than that and you're probably ruminating—a second-semester word for worrying.

Constructive thought and worry are entirely different processes.

Worry has little if any value and usually involves going over and over the facts and possible outcomes of your dilemma of the moment until you have created a cerebral house of mirrors. Even if you manage to hit upon a solution, if you're in a worry mode you'll come up with all sorts of objections to the solution. At this point, you are under an all-out siege from your gremlin. Worrying is not fun, and it's bad for your health. When next you worry, notice how it feels. Your breathing will be shallow, your brow will be furrowed, and your body will feel tense in those places your gremlin thinks are most vulnerable.

If you are into less than healthy ways of managing your stress, such as smoking, excessive drinking, or overeating, your gremlin will tempt you with these behaviors and then taunt you for engaging in them. Your gremlin is not a cute character or a whimsical concept. Your gremlin is a force within you that is out to destroy you. He can do so by perpetuating worry. The experience of worry is uncomfortable and destructive.

Worry is laced with anxiety and fraught with anguish. It grows out of a preoccupation with fears about the future, unwillingness to release the past, and/or a refusal to accept what is obvious in the here and now. Constructive thinking, on the other hand, begins with a willingness to look yourself and your situation squarely in the eye. It requires relaxed concentration, the ability to control your awareness, and telling yourself the truth. It is sometimes inspired by anxiety but is never dominated by it.

Constructive thinking requires an awareness of where you are and the notion of where you want to be. It entails a review of possible resources; a sensitivity to potential snafus; and at least a rough plan for using your resources to leap over, circumvent, or bust through the stumbling blocks to your goal.

Can one's gremlin really be tamed?

Absolutely. The Gremlin-Taming Method is tried and true. But taming your gremlin is not a once-and-for-all-time kind of deal. That's why the Gremlin-Taming Method requires that you always be in process. Contentment and peace of mind are not entities to be captured once and for all. Doing so is a breath-to-breath activity, at which, if you practice the method and take it to heart, you will get really good—so good that your gremlin's bullying and berating, his ominous threats, and his hypnotic whispers will become completely inconsequential.

What is the relationship between psychotherapy and gremlin-taming?

Any personal growth experience—whether it's called psychotherapy, counseling, coaching, or consultation—if it is to be truly effective, must get down to what I think of as gremlin-taming. Resolving inner duality is the bottom line when it comes to getting on with and relishing one's existence.

Do you object to traditional psychotherapy?

Not at all. There are many wonderful psychotherapists out there. It's a myth that most psychotherapists spend their time delving into their clients' pasts, ferreting out and analyzing reasons for maladaptive thoughts and actions. That is simply not true of all psychotherapists. There are many wonderful psychotherapists who work existentially and phenomenologically, and there are many wonderful psychoanalysts.

What I object to is bad psychotherapy. I object to the fact that literally millions of people out there are accepting labels of mental illness and taking medicine to cope with life's transitions and the emotional ups and downs that are a natural byproduct of being human and suffering the whips and scorns of time. It's been suggested that some of the world's largest drug companies "brand" conditions just as they "brand" medicines, by using three strategies: giving a little-known condition new attention; renaming an existing disease; or creating a whole new illness. Dr. David Henry, professor of clinical pharmacology at Newcastle University, calls this "disease mongering," the practice of turning ordinary life and behavior into medical illness to expand the market for drugs and other products. This practice is driving up health care costs for all of us, and it is making health insurance prohibitive for many.

I've been in practice since 1972 and have seen that there is always a popular malady of the day. Currently, it is bipolar disorder. By the time this book hits the shelves, I have no idea what it will be. A few years back, untold numbers of people were being told that they *had* depression (as opposed to depressing themselves). Before that, masses were labeled as alcoholic or codependent. I've had clients who were genuine, first-rate victims of bipolar disorder, anxiety, and depression. It's not a pretty picture. These are serious and unfortunate states of being, and I find it disturbing that these days there are so many amateurs out there claiming the title.

But isn't bipolar disorder a biochemical imbalance, and isn't that true of depression as well?

Of course these things are biochemical. Being sad is biochemical. So is being angry, and getting an erection, and jumping for joy. Every experience we have is to some extent biochemical. We're chemical beings.

My point is this: in our obsessive quest to make life predictable and pain free, we keep narrowing the parameters of what we consider normal, and by imposing an increasingly rigid standard of normalcy, we're demanding a level of homogeneity that is destructive to individuals and society. Someone who steps outside the boundaries of our little homogeneous bubble is considered deviant or sick, and therefore in need of medication or treatment (another word for "fixing"). This certainly

46

discourages creative living. Worse yet, it releases people from taking responsibility for their own bad choices.

Gremlin-taming sounds like a cute metaphor for something you obviously take quite seriously. Do you think this dampens your mystique and dilutes your message?

If I thought I had even a modicum of mystique, believe me, I'd do nothing to dampen it. Regarding "cute," I don't want to appear harsh or judgmental, but where gremlin-taming is concerned, I'd like to take "cute," tie it down spread-eagle, and jump up and down on it with both feet until it begs for mercy. Then I'd jump on it some more until it had no breath left.

I apologize for the digression. I gotta be me. It's part of my mystique.

Look. Gremlin-taming might not be the sort of terminology that floats your boat—maybe it's too whimsical-sounding. In 1983 when I first wrote *Taming Your Gremlin*, I must have considered twenty-five titles and metaphors. Going through old files, I recently came across a short list. Would you have been more likely to climb on board if you had encountered one of these?

"Endarkenment: Accentuating the Obvious and the Existential Theory of Change"

"The Art of Graceful Change"

"A Road Map to Emotional Self-Sufficiency"

"Becoming Mindless: The Path to Mindfulness"

"The Basics of Pleasure"

"Leading with Your Heart"

"The Carson Method."

(A group of my advanced trainees came up with that last one. I overplayed my "Aw, shucks, it's not about me," and they essentially said, "Yeah, you're right," and there went my shot at name recognition.)

But hey. The word is not the thing, nor is the description the described, right? However, given that you and I have chosen to communicate via my writing and your reading, words are about all we got. I say, let's stick with "gremlin-taming." The phrase has come to mean a lot to me and a few hundred thousand other folks in a cross-section of cultures and circumstances. What matters is, the method works, and we're here to learn, right?

What would you say are the key principles of the Gremlin-Taming Method?

This was Doug's final question to me, and it's a good one. It's a topic I've spoken about often, and for our purposes here and now, I'd like to take a little time to elaborate on it and recommend some specific reading to you.

There are sixteen key principles in the Gremlin-Taming Method. Nine of them are covered in *Taming Your Gremlin* (though nowhere in that work do I say, "These are the first nine principles of gremlin-taming").

It is quite important to remember, though, as the often-used adage reminds us, "The whole is different from the sum of the parts." Better yet, "There's no substitute for experience." Even better yet, "There is a difference between techniques and technique."

You can read about the techniques of mountain biking, sailing, or flying a jet until you're a walking, talking encyclopedia on how to propel each, but until you develop a feel for the bike, boat, or plane, you're in for a tension-filled inner experience and a rugged ride. The same is true for gremlin-taming.

Gremlin-taming is not a philosophy. It is a skill set, the benefits of which expand exponentially and unfold continually as one practices the method. "Practice" is the key word here.

THE BASICS OF PLEASURE

The first six principles of the Gremlin-Taming Method are called the Basics of Pleasure. These six principles constitute a method for establishing, and when necessary restoring, one's emotional equilibrium, one's sense of centeredness, even in the midst of outrageous upheaval. When practiced, they yield a strong sense of clarity, emotional self-sufficiency, and a healthy sense of detachment from circumstances.

1. **Make being centered and feeling good a top priority.**
   (page 38, *Taming Your Gremlin*, revised edition)

2. **Remember that doing so is primarily an inside job.**
   (page 40, *Taming Your Gremlin*)

3. **Notice where you end and all else begins—the miraculous sheath known as your skin.**
   (pages 31–32, *Taming Your Gremlin*)

4. **Breathe, dammit, breathe.**
   (pages 32–35, *Taming Your Gremlin*)

5. **Relax your pact to keep your act intact.**
   (pages 70–85, *Taming Your Gremlin*)

6. **Establish the Here and Now as your home base, from which you consciously direct your spotlight of awareness.**
   (pages 35–39, *Taming Your Gremlin*)

Key words regarding the Basics of Pleasure are balance, independence, emotional self-sufficiency, healthy detachment.

But you and I want more than balance, independence, emotional self-sufficiency, and a healthy sense of detachment from circumstances. What good are they if we don't have one other important element? Freedom. That's where the next three principles, known as the Art of Graceful Change, come in.

THE ART OF GRACEFUL CHANGE

The Art of Graceful Change is a three-step process for free-ing yourself from your Hypnotic Pre-Convictions (HPCs), your outdated Habitual Behavior Patterns (HBPs), and your gremlin's chatter. The Art of Graceful Change is a method for continually cleansing the channel between your soul and your persona, that is, between your Heart and your actions. It is a method for getting a sliver of light between who you really are and your limiting ideas *about* who you are. These three principles combine to form the road map that is the heart of gremlin-taming. Here they are:

7. **Simply noticing**
   (pages 7–10, *Taming Your Gremlin*, revised edition)

8. **Playing with options**
   (pages 108–129, *Taming Your Gremlin*)

9. **Being in process**
   (pages 164–165, *Taming Your Gremlin*)

Key words regarding the Art of Graceful Change are aware-ness, choice, experimentation, freedom.

And there's more. Even if you are, at any point, in balance, in touch with your emotional self-sufficiency, and free from the encumbrance of Hypnotic Pre-Convictions (HPCs), Habitual Behavior Patterns (HBPs), and gremlin chatter, you would be wise to acknowledge that you are, indeed, *interdependent* with all and everything.

Like any organism, you are a functional whole, a system, part of an endless network of larger functional, interrelated systems—bigger than the universe and smaller than your eye can witness. Like it or not, we're all in this thing together, which brings us to the next seven principles in the Gremlin-Taming Method: Creating Rewarding Relationships.

Chapter 12

Creating Rewarding Relationships

There is an acronym I adore. It is I CREATE. I am enamored of it for two reasons: first, because following the strategy hidden within it has greatly enriched my life, and second, because I made it up.

I CREATE is a checklist for making certain you are doing your part to maximize the rewards inherent in any breath's worth of time. It's a way of living life as a meditation, a system for realizing the sacredness of every moment. And it is a road map for forming and sustaining productive, vibrant relationships with "all and everything."

Every kind word that comes your way, every pat on the back, every dollar you receive comes to you from somebody. Every business that touches your life, every organization you are a part of—even your family—is simply a network of people: people in relationships.

And you live entwined in networks of relationships, not just with people and other breathing things but with all realms of mind and matter and matters of the mind. You have relationships with your thoughts, your memories, your Heart, your energy, your fantasies; with money and music and missing pieces, with plans and possibilities. The quality of your life and the quality of your relationships are inextricably linked.

What does I CREATE stand for? My initial idea was to have you wait for the complete answer to that question. I was going to slowly unfold the words in the acronym by writing chapters titled as each of the seven keys and explicating each of them. I envisioned offering you a delicate banquet of seven courses (chapters) of poignant prose, each a superbly blended fusion of textures and tastiness, each piquancy complementing the preceding one and the next to come. Your intellectual taste buds would scream with joy after each serving, yet be tinged with titillating anticipation of the next. Then it occurred to me: You may be like me and have the attention span of a three-year-old, which, of course, means that you would thumb through the book, rushing to dessert, as it were, noting the title of each chapter, and therefore learning every word that I CREATE stands for.

I could, of course, remind you on every page or two not to do that, but again, if your attention span is like mine, it would be like trying to smuggle daylight past a rooster. So here are the seven words:

INTENTION

CONNECTION

RESPECT

ENVIRONMENT

AUTHENTICITY

TRUST

EXPERIENCE

Chapter 13

Intention

In every moment you are a devotee. In every breath's worth of time you devote your life to something. You do so via your awareness.

Your awareness is a spotlight placed on a pedestal in the present moment. From its base in the moment called Now, you control it. You can focus it with the precision of a laser, or broaden it, drawing into your consciousness all manner of facts, fantasies, and fantastic goings-on. You can shift it slowly from people to possibilities, or let it flit from notion to notion, from thought to thought, from prop to player. It can lead you, or you can lead it. In relation to your *spotlight of awareness*, you can be a passenger or a driver, a victim or a participant, a pawn or a player.

Your *spotlight of awareness* belongs to you. It's a gift, and it's here with you now. Breath to breath, consciously or unconsciously, you choose where to shine it. You are doing so in this moment, and in this one as well. And in this one, too. Paying attention—that is, consciously focusing your awareness—is a gentle process, and it's a pleasure. "Consciously" is a key word here. After all, you've been shining that spotlight of awareness all around for years, and sometimes you've done it consciously. But what if you did so with more consciousness? Sharper attention? A clearer Intention? Imagine the possibilities. Imagine how you would feel, and note:

How you feel, your inner experience,
breath to breath, is the quintessential measure
of the quality of your existence.

Every experience you have in this life occurs within the boundary defined by your skin. Events occur around you, and some include you, but your experience of these events occurs within the boundary defined by your skin. Within that boundary lie your thoughts, your concepts, your imaginings, your memories, your emotions, and all the physical sensations you experience, from a pleasing taste to a warm breeze on your skin to hardly bearable pain.

From within that boundary, you are drawing in my words. In there, you interpret and define your reality. You give it meaning. You spice it up, and you tone it down. You embellish and diminish. You drag in your past and your thoughts about the future. From within that boundary, you may choose to cast your spotlight of awareness onto your present surroundings. Onto a person, maybe—her movements, her facial expressions, her voice. The quality of attention you pay is completely up to you. You can watch, you can listen, you might sneak a glance or boldly peruse, eavesdrop or say, "Please speak louder," turn away or turn toward.

As a small boy in a small town in West Texas, I often played outside and out of my mother's sight. I'd be completely caught up in the illusion that I was a gunfighter or a pirate when her voice would drift into my ears from our back porch. "Richard, what are you up to?" Usually, without interrupting my play, I yelled back, "Nothin'." Clearly, it was not the poetic articulation of my current activity she was after, but rather the sound of my voice and the assurance that I was alive. She'd simply say, "Okay." And that was that.

But now that I think about it, it's a great question to ask yourself moment to moment. What *are* you up to? What *are* you doing with your precious breath's worth of time? And what did you do with the last few? And how about the next one hundred or so?

Your Intention is different from your desires, goals, wants, and needs. You may desire her favor, want to win the big game, or long to have naturally curly hair or big biceps. But Intention is a moment-to-moment thing. Your Intention is to pay *attention*. To what? That's up to you. With every breath, it's up to you. What do you want to devote your attention to right now?

In any moment, there's a lot going on. Right now, for example. I see my beautiful black-and-white cat, Sophie, sleeping on the sofa. I hear the fireplace crackling on my right, and out of the corner of my eye I see it flicker. I feel the texture of the paper and my pen on the paper. Now, I'm feeling restless. Now, I'm wondering about your present experience. There's Sophie again. She's curled up, and her paws are over her eyes. I want to go pet her. I'll be right back.

She loved it. Me, too. A lot going on. Sights, sounds, scents, things to touch and taste, physical sensations, thoughts, fantasies, and memories. In each moment a wealth of experiences is available to each of the six and a half billion of us, and in each moment each of us chooses what to make important. We each decide, consciously or unconsciously, moment to moment, what to bring into the foreground of our experience and what to relegate to background.

*In each moment you choose what gift
to bring to your Heart.*

Breath to breath, you organize your own reality by bringing into your foreground what you deem important and relegating to the background of your experience that which you deem less important. In any breath's worth of time, you decide, consciously or unconsciously, to what or to whom you wish to devote your attention. You decide what to present to your Heart.

When forming your reality, if you have a clear Intention about what you want to focus on, you will create a sharp distinction between the foreground of your current experience and the background. The result will be excitement. That excitement will be felt as a tiny vibration or a warm feeling in your Heart.

It might not be whoop-and-holler excitement, but it will indeed be excitement—vibrancy, the vibrancy that makes life's rich moments rich. If, on the other hand, your Intention is not clear, and you broaden your spotlight of awareness, bringing in too much at once, with nothing in sharp focus, you will feel spacey, or in a fog. This is not always an unpleasant experience.

Withdrawal from intense contact is inevitable and necessary if you are to replenish your energy so that you can again fully engage with whatever or whomever you choose. The novel you are reading in bed may be stimulating, but there is a point at which you are sated with it and ready for a snooze. The distinction between the background and foreground of your experience gets fuzzy, and then you crater. This happens to you in subtler ways, all day long, and all life long.

Think of how a newborn or infant focuses in for a few minutes, then you see the baby's eyelids flicker and the gaze soften as the sharpness of the baby's focus lessens. From birth through adulthood, consciously or unconsciously, we play with our inner spotlight of awareness. Learning to do so with a clearer and clearer intention is a lifelong process. Gracefully regulating the flow of your awareness between intense contact and withdrawal is one of the keys to staying calm, collected, and content.

Just as blurring the distinction between the background and the foreground of your experience can result in a spacey feeling, so shifting the foreground of your experience rapidly, without fully attending to any one thing, can result in your feeling scattered, confused, or overwhelmed. When you skip rapidly from place to place, thing to thing, possibility to possibility, you don't give your Heart time to resonate with any one aspect of your experience.

Scarlett came to see me saying, "I am a nervous wreck, and I can't cope with the stress in my life." As we talked it quickly became apparent to me that Scarlett skittered through life like a firefly in heat, continually finding new projects to take on. The mother of two elementary school-age children, Scarlett was active in the PTA, was a Girl Scout Troop leader, served on the board of a community center, and participated in Hadassah. Her breathing was shallow, and it, and her speech, were rapid. Her head and mouth worked like a gumball machine with the little trapdoor stuck open. Thoughts left her brain and rolled out of her mouth, seemingly uninhibited by forethought.

She chattered like a magpie in our first session. She interrupted me almost every time I spoke, and gave no indication that she had any interest in my words. She wasn't overtly rude, just absorbed with her own thoughts, each one often only barely related to the former thought or the next, but for an underlying theme: that her life was completely torturous because she had so much more to handle than anyone else on the planet, and that doing so was especially hard, given her "health problems"—mainly that she was tired constantly, and every few weeks or so she was so exhausted that she stayed in bed for a day or two. She added that her health problems had medical science stumped but that she would keep on trucking through her misery.

As it turned out, underneath Scarlett's "Harried Martyr" act, she really was one of the loveliest souls I've ever encountered. Her primary Hypnotic Pre-Conviction was that being overwhelmed, with far too much to do, and suffering through

58

it, was noble. It made one a "good person." It was a long-standing HPC she had gulped down from watching her mama. And that HPC was stacked right on top of another closely related one: "Unless I'm scurrying around, knocking myself out, I have no value. In fact, I don't know what to do with myself, or even who I am." Scarlett was more of a human "doing" than a human being. She knew virtually nothing about simply connecting in the present moment.

I helped Scarlett begin to *simply notice* her breathing and her internal tempo, how she used her words to advertise her act, and the HPCs on which her attachment to her act was based. I helped her to do so in our relationship, and asked that she do so between our sessions as well. I asked that between our sessions she *simply notice* the general ratio of time between her use of her mouth and her use of her ears, what topics she chose to speak to others about, her breathing, how she spent time, and her use of her eyes. I emphasized that she should not try to change a thing, but rather *simply notice*. She asked if she could take notes on what she noticed, and I said that was up to her.

In our next session, Scarlett's breathing was notably slower and deeper. In brief, she reported that she had noticed between our last session and this one that she used her mouth far more than her ears, that she tended to talk mostly about her ailments and how much she had to do, that she talked on the phone a lot, that she kept forgetting to notice her breathing, and that when she did it was very shallow. But she wasn't sure about her eyes. I told her I had noticed that she shifted them often and rarely looked directly at me for any length of time. When I said this, Scarlett's breathing became very shallow. I asked her if she would be willing to do an experiment with me, and she said, "Like what?" her eyes darting around the room. I said, "Keep your breathing as it is, and keep looking around the room and do not look directly at me." She said that would be easy, and she did as I asked for a minute or so. She then looked right at me and said she wanted to stop.

She sounded almost angry, but her gaze was steady, and her breathing a little bit deeper. I asked how she felt. Looking directly at me, she said, simply, "Okay."

I asked what her experience had been while she was doing the experiment. She said that she felt awkward and that the whole thing was contrived. I asked, "What is your objection to being contrived?" She answered, "I don't like it. I want to be real." I said, "Say that again." She said, "I want to be real." I asked her to continue looking me directly in the eye and say it again, slowly. She did, and began to smile slightly. I asked her to again say the phrase slowly, and to feel every word. She did, and not only did she feel every word, so did I. I then asked Scarlett to relax her breathing, making sure to take in all the air she wanted, and to slowly look around my office. I encouraged her to notice the view through the floor-to-ceiling windows, as well. I told her it was okay if she walked around to do so. I again reminded her to keep her breathing relaxed and clear, and suggested that she slowly shift her awareness back and forth between her breathing and her visual field, bypassing her intellect and simply noticing objects and shadows and light.

As she moved around the office I walked with her. I reminded her several times to attend to her breathing, and to be sure to take in all the air she wanted, and to exhale fully. After several moments of slowly strolling and looking and breathing comfortably, Scarlett began to look more relaxed and present than I had previously seen her. Eventually, she looked at me with the same gentle gaze with which she was observing my office and the beautiful creek and trees outside. I was struck by the vibrancy of her presence as she looked me lovingly in the eye and said, "Hello. It's nice to see you."

Being harried is a way of avoiding making clear, purposeful contact. Often people who play harried are starved for intimacy but haven't a clue how to connect—probably because, as a child, they got more attention for doing than being. Talk about fertile ground for gremlin activity. This is a perfect set-up for chatter such as this:

"You'll never do enough, or be enough."

"Who you are is less important than what you do."

"Put yourself last, or at least second."

It's sad but true. In some families, a particularly cruel gremlin myth is passed down from generation to generation—the notion that suffering and feeling overwhelmed is somehow noble. Being harried can become a game.

People who play harried do so as a way of announcing to others and proving to themselves that they are worthy and noble, as demonstrated by their willingness to suffer; and that others in the world have no right to be upset with them, as demonstrated by the fact that they are trying so very hard; and that screwups are not their fault, as demonstrated by the fact that "no one could possibly straighten out this mess or get all of this done." Some folks, like Scarlett, are professionals at playing harried. The rest of us are harried on occasion in spite of knowing better.

When together folks like you and me feel hassled and harried, our breathing is shallow and fast, our heartbeat is rapid, and we perspire, if only slightly. We look coyote-eyed, and we feel like gnawing on leather. When habitual hard-core "harriedites" do it, they too look frantic, but with a forlorn, pitiful tint.

To modify your own occasional fits of frenetic fervor, first catch yourself in the act and ask yourself, "What, Dear One, are you trying to prove?" Form a clear Intention about what you would like to spend your next few breaths of time connecting with—that is, what you'd like to bring into the foreground of your experience. Sounds simple? It is. But it isn't easy. You may be thinking, "But I have ADD."

Pretend you don't. Let go of your ADD HPC. Come on—

pretend. Just like the time you played Barbie, or cowboys and Indians. Play as if you don't have ADD. Then, place your awareness on your breathing for a few breaths, taking in all the air you want, and exhaling fully. Notice the path of your breath as you inhale and as you exhale, remembering that your Heart wants you to give it the time and space to experience. And remember, too:

There is no positive cause-and-effect correlation between being harried and getting a job done expediently and effectively.

Breathe. Get your Intention clear about what you want to attend to. Attend only to it.

A word about multitasking. In the purest sense, there really is no such thing. You can't be two places at once, so quit trying. You can learn to switch what is in your foreground rather quickly and smoothly if you would like, but really attending to two things at once? No way. Don't play harried.

In any moment your Intention is to pay attention to something. Ask yourself precisely what you want to attend to next, and for how long. Think of your life as an opportunity to provide your Heart with experiences. Think of your breathing as a metronome that you will use to regulate the tempo of the flow of your awareness. Your challenge is to set the metronome at a tempo that allows you to accomplish whatever you want to accomplish at the speed you choose, while still "breathing easy" and having your Heart enjoy the process. You can use your metronome to set a pace for activities as physically demanding as competitive cycling or running, or for intensely intellectually demanding activities such as mastering a Saturday *New York Times* crossword puzzle.

If you'd like to experiment with getting a feel for how to set your internal metronome, I suggest that you first think of an activity you want to perform without getting harried, such as cleaning your house when you learn unexpected visitors are on their way. Use your dominant hand to draw a sideways figure eight in the air, like this:

The sideways figure eight should be about chest high and a little wider than the width of your shoulders from tip to tip. Form the figure eight in the air in a continuous motion. (Don't try this while holding a glass of V8 and wearing your favorite T-shirt.) As you make your figure eight, experiment with different speeds of doing so. Find a speed for your hand that is compatible with the pace you want to move in order to comfortably and expediently perform whatever task you have in mind. Notice that you can move your hand really rapidly, yet smoothly. And notice, too, that even if your hand moves quite swiftly, you can keep your breathing relaxed, full, and easy.

MORE ON THE MIND

Ever felt as if you had missed something? As if you were there physically, but now that you reflect on the event, you realize that your body was there but you missed the experience? Sure you have. And you said all the right things. You did exactly as those little pictures in your head said you should—and now, you have in your head somewhere pictures of the event itself. Many are faded; some you like; some you don't. All are one-dimensional.

Mired in your mind, you miss a lot. You remember the look on your child's face at the recital, but were you present enough at the time to notice the warm feeling in your Heart as you looked at her? You may recall your mother's sobs at the death of a beloved family member or friend, and remember touching her shoulder, but what stopped you from taking her face in your hands and looking her in the eye? Your Heart would have liked that, but your mind got in the way. You miss a lot when you're lost in your mind. Your Heart wants you to fully experience your existence moment to moment, not to hide out in the warehouse of the mind. To trust your Heart is to be brave. To hide out in your mind is to be a chicken-shit.

What did his lips on your cheek really feel like? Were you in touch with the longing to rush to the rescue when your youngest looked scared and unsure? What about the sensation when that special one first looked you in the eye and said, "I really love you?" Did you feel it deeply enough to connect with it? Have you really been present enough to feel the thrill of a tough job completed well, or the incomparable feeling of satisfaction born from the kudos of your peers? Snapshots are nice, but the firsthand Heart experience is fulfilling. Experience has its own language, and it is not the language of the mind.

Your mind is yours to use, to be enjoyed, to remember, to fantasize, to analyze, to rehearse for the future. But to let it unknowingly contaminate the richness of your moment-to-moment experience is a shame. It is a deadening of you, a miniature suicide.

You literally have a choice all day long, with every breath's worth of time, whether to be in the world or in the world of mind.

REALMS OF AWARENESS

At any point, your spotlight of awareness is in one of three realms: your body, your present surroundings, or the world of mind.

Your body begins deep inside with your breathing and ends at the outer limits of your skin. Your present surroundings include all you can experience using your sensory receptors—a taste or scent or sight or sound or something your skin touches.

To *simply notice* your experience of your body is to *be here, now*. To *simply notice* your present surroundings is to *be here, now*. To interpret, analyze, fantasize, or remember takes you into the world of mind.

Your mind holds within it memories, fantasies, and analytical thoughts. Within your mind you may recall a reality so vividly sometimes that you reexperience the emotions and the physical sensations of the past event. Within your mind you may fantasize happenings so vividly that you feel excitement or fear or joy or sadness or anger. Your mind is rich with limitless possibilities. Entered with Intention, consciousness, and choice, your mind is an infinite wonderland. Entered unknowingly, it can contaminate, corrupt, distort, and/or even embellish the gift of true experience.

Play within your mind. Enjoy it. Enter it at will. But do so with a clear Intention. Stay conscious of the flow of your awareness and of your intentional choice about where to place your awareness, lest you drift in and out of your mind unknowingly and thereby forgo your pure experience of your very own life as it is unfolding for you right here and right now—and totally missing your Heart.

And remember, lurking in the shadows of your mind is your gremlin, the monster of the mind. He's always waiting for the opportunity to seduce you away from the richness of pure experience and from your Heart.

When you encounter your gremlin, you'll know it—if, that is, you're attending to your breathing. Your breathing will become shallow, and you will begin to manifest tension in your body—your shoulders, perhaps, or your jaws, or your stomach, or your back. You may notice that your brow is furrowed. Your gremlin will invite you into a horror movie composed of catastrophic expectations or fears, or invite you to watch his favorite program on the History Channel—the one called Regrets. Or perhaps he'll simply whisper HPCs to you about who you are and how the world works, diverting you from the freshness of new experience and from the excitement inherent in the unpredictability of all and everything.

You may *simply notice* the monster of your mind as soon as he appears and attempts to engage you, or you may not become aware of him until you're enmeshed in an intimate encounter with him. Either way is fine. There's nothing to fear. Your gremlin is no match for you. You are never more than a breath or two away from returning to your home base in the Here and Now and from reconnecting with your Heart.

Simply notice your gremlin. *Play with Options* (pages 108–132, revised edition of *Taming Your Gremlin*), and *Be in Process*. To try to force him to leave or to try to *force* yourself to turn away from him will merely induce tension. Remember, gremlin-taming requires effort, but not strain. To work against what is, merely sets up resistance. It creates a duality, a wrestling match between you and your gremlin, in which you will become more entangled with him, not less.

Instead of wrestling with your gremlin, bring him into the light by relaxing your breathing and *simply noticing* his chatter. Then, make a relaxed choice to spend a few moments with him or to gently redirect your awareness. Should you decide to spend time engaged with him, set a clear Intention to do so. Get into it. Listen to his rants, raves, put-downs, fear tactics, resentments, regrets, and Hypnotic Pre-Convictions—but stay at choice with doing so, by establishing a clear Intention.

I suggest setting a predetermined time limit for such encounters. One or two minutes is more than enough time. Literally, look at your watch and set a time limit. When your time is up, redirect your awareness to your body (your breathing, perhaps), to your immediate surroundings. Or, if you prefer, stay in the world of mind, but change channels. Your mind contains an infinite number of channels. Whatever you choose to attend to, do so with a clear Intention.

How about a break? Let's take a walk.

AN INTENTIONAL STROLL
(A WALKING MEDITATION)

Plan a time when you can block out at least thirty minutes. More time would be terrific.

Okay, you're about to take a leisurely walk. You might think of this walk as an opportunity to provide your Heart with some good times. It's also an opportunity to listen to your Heart—to see what experiences it wants more of. Get to a setting, preferably outside, that you find pleasant. Once you are in a setting you enjoy, stand for a moment with your eyes closed, or at least half closed, and your awareness on your breathing. Simply notice your breathing and the area in the center of your chest around and behind your physical heart. Exhale fully, and as you inhale make certain to take in all the air your body wants. Begin, then, to inhale and exhale at a pace that is comfortable for you. Breathe naturally. But again, make certain that you take in all the air your body desires and that you exhale fully.

Make your breathing the foreground of your experience for several breaths. Then, for a few breaths, gently allow your breathing to become background, and allow the surface of your skin to become the foreground of your experience. Allow your awareness to drift back and forth between your breathing and your skin.

Now, gently lift your eyelids and begin to stroll. As you stroll, consciously and gently shift your *spotlight of awareness* from your breathing to some aspect of your present surroundings. Notice what's available to you via your sensory receptors—sights, sounds, scents. Intentionally select what you want to bring into your foreground and what you want to relegate to background. Walk slowly and gently, but with clear Intention guide your *spotlight of awareness*. Frequently, return your awareness to your breathing for a breath or two, perhaps even stopping and dropping your eyelids to do so. Take in all the air you

67

want, and exhale fully. Attend also to the feeling of air on your skin and clothes on your skin.

Experiment with making your sensory experience your main event. Experiment, too, with gently shifting the foreground of your experience. You might, for example, bring several leaves of a tree into your foreground, and relegate the rest of the tree, as well as the light and shadows behind the leaves, into your background. Or shift your awareness so that the entire tree becomes the foreground of your experience and all else becomes background. Or stand comfortably, close your eyes, and attend to sounds drifting in through your ears. Notice the feeling of your feet on the ground (performing this intentional walk barefoot can be a delightful experience). Periodically, re-notice your breathing and the surface of your skin.

Walking in this fashion for even ten or fifteen minutes can refresh you for hours. You can actually practice walking meditation anywhere as a way of re-centering yourself, establishing the current moment as your home base and your breathing as the anchor of your experience. From time to time you might even choose to relegate both your breathing and your present surroundings to the background of your experience and simply notice the meanderings of your mind.

You can play with many variations of a walking meditation, including focusing less on your surroundings and more on the motion of your body, attending to the shift of your weight as you stroll and to the movement of your arms and legs. Remember:

At any point, you are a devotee.

At any point, you choose where to place your awareness.

Your Intention is to make a Connection.

What does this have to do with gremlin-taming?

Everything. When *Taming Your Gremlin* was first published by Harper & Row (now HarperCollins), the subtitle was *A Guide to Enjoying Yourself*, and that, quite simply, is what gremlin-taming is all about. It's a worthy endeavor. François-Marie Arouet, better known as Voltaire, put it this way: "Pleasure is the object of all rational creatures." Voltaire had a way of cutting out the deadwood. And, I hasten to add, enjoying yourself is synonymous with getting out of your own way (the subtitle of the revised edition of *Taming Your Gremlin*), so that you can have an unabashed, uncompromising, all-out experience of yourself and the world in which you live.

Your gremlin is hell-bent on having you miss this pleasure. Why this is so, I haven't a clue. But show me someone who claims to be gremlin free, and I'll show you a humanoid "out o' touch." Even the grandest teachers, including those known as masters, have come face-to-face with their own internal saboteurs. Jesus wrestled with his in the desert. Buddha attained enlightenment only after overcoming the attack and temptations of Mara, "The Evil One." Even Freud gave these internal nemeses a nod when he said, "No one who conjures up the most evil of the half-tamed demons that inhabit the human beast and seeks to wrestle with them can expect to come through the struggle unscathed."

A lot of folks jump to the conclusion that their gremlin is their negative thoughts, painful past experiences, regrets, and fears. Nope. These are all weapons in his arsenal, but, remember, your gremlin is your gremlin by virtue of his Intention, and his Intention is to dampen your joy and render your life completely meaningless and miserable. Your gremlin is NOT cute (don't get me started). Sure, he'll use all the above tactics, but his first line of attack is simply to lull you into unconsciousness—that is, to have you completely space out and forget that your primary Intention (survival excepted) is to enjoy your existence, breath to breath, and that doing so is synonymous with fully connecting with what is going on within you and what is going on around you.

Your gremlin is determined to have you forget that your Intention is to provide your Heart with a beautiful experience in each breath's worth of time by forming a solid, moment-to-moment Connection.

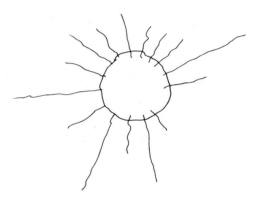

Chapter 14

Connection

Have you ever tried to have a conversation with someone who was engrossed in a television program or been talking with someone at a gathering when he or she was preoccupied with visually scanning the room? If so, you weren't fooled, were you? Those people were cheating not just you but themselves and their Heart out of a rich opportunity for Connection.

Remember how we discussed that in every moment you're a devotee? That is, you devote your *spotlight of awareness* to something. It's true. In any moment, you choose, consciously or unconsciously, to pay attention to something, and you control the quality of attention you pay.

The quality of your relationships depends in great part on the quality of the contact you make, and the quality of your contact hinges on a clear Intention. In creating rewarding relationships, your Intention must be to pay *attention*, to connect. The "C" in I CREATE stands for Connection.

A USEFUL CONTINUUM

Let's create a continuum. At one end of the continuum, see yourself as frightened—under attack. Picture yourself hunkered down in a corner, trying to cover yourself up with your hands and arms as if to protect yourself from an attacker. Your breathing is cramped and shallow. You're tensing your body in anticipation of pain, and your energy is pulling inward. Think of this image as an exaggerated version of how you may sometimes feel in relationships: insecure, scared, and uptight.

At the other end of the continuum, create a picture of yourself standing with your feet parallel and shoulder-width apart, your arms hanging comfortably to your sides, your breathing clear and relaxed as you gently guide your awareness back and forth between your breathing and your immediate surroundings. You're feeling centered, alert, and unguarded. You are, as the late Fritz Perls might say, creatively indifferent—open to experience without judgment or expectations. You are providing your Heart a pure, in-the-moment experience.

At any point, you place yourself somewhere on an imaginary continuum bounded by these two extremes: scrunched up with your breathing shallow and your energy turned inward, or open, relaxed, and available to enjoy. You are placing yourself on the continuum now, and you do so, consciously or unconsciously, in every waking moment of your day. The decision about where to place yourself along this continuum at any moment is completely your choice.

Want to have a big time? Start *simply noticing* where, moment to moment, situation to situation, you place yourself on this continuum. In a day's time, in all likelihood, you will find all manner of folks in front of you. Big people, little people, those you enjoy, those you aren't so sure about. And you will encounter them under a wide range of circumstances. You'll have lots of opportunities to experiment. Lovers, friends, kids, colleagues, your friendly grocer.

In each fresh encounter, notice where you place yourself on the imaginary continuum. Note: "imaginary." Don't actually assume either of the two extreme postures, or you could be carted away to one of those psychiatric facilities that have sprung up like wild onions. Pay special attention to your Heart—that is, to the center of your chest—and to your breathing. If your chest is tight or your breathing is shallow, you are placing yourself toward the uptight end of the continuum. This is neither good nor bad, but in all likelihood making yourself uptight in most instances is no more than a Habitual Behavior Pattern (HBP) born of an outdated belief—a Hypnotic Pre-Conviction (HPC).

Should you notice that you've placed yourself at the uptight end of the continuum, ask yourself a simple question: What, Dear One, are you afraid of? And notice the answer that comes into your head. You needn't analyze it or try to figure out its origin. Simply notice the uptightness and the answer to your question. Trust your first-level thought here.

First-level thought is a simple process of gently reflecting on any given topic during a couple of full, easy, and complete breaths. It's a superior alternative to worrying, and at times it can serve you even better than in-depth constructive thought. While in-depth constructive thought has an important place in your life, there are many times when first-level thought will simply prove more efficient (for instance, when you're selecting what restaurant to go to). It saves a lot of time. You may not always make the perfect decision, but you save lots of precious breaths' worth of time.

First-level thought involves trusting your innate ability to come up with usable information quickly and effortlessly. It is especially valuable in learning about yourself and getting in touch with your most fundamental preferences, and for witnessing your HPCs about yourself and about how the world works.

The answer to "What, Dear One, are you afraid of?" may be as simple as

73

"I'm afraid he or she won't like me."

or

"He'll yell at me."

or

"They'll laugh at me."

or

"She might leave me."

Simply noticing your first-level thought is plenty, because it kicks into action the Zen Theory of Change. Here it is again:

I free myself

not by trying to free myself

but by *simply noticing* how I am imprisoning myself

in the very moment in which I am imprisoning myself.

PLAYING WITH OPTIONS

If you'd like, you might PLAY with an option, such as accentuating the uptightness by making your breathing even more shallow and increasing the tightness in your chest and/or accentuating the answer to your "What, Dear One, are you afraid of?" question.

"She'll see how stupid I am. I'll make a fool of myself. She'll tell all her friends, and they'll gossip about me and make fun of me and have a big time at my expense. I've never been any good at making new friends. I think I'll go home and stay in the house and never come out again."

74

You'll quickly get to the point of absurdity. Even if what you're saying to yourself has a ring of truth to it and isn't absurd, what will become clearly absurd is that you are spending precious moments of your finite life making yourself miserable. Remember the thumb-in-the-eye routine?

Or, here's another option to play with if you catch yourself at the uptight end of your imaginary continuum. In *Taming Your Gremlin*, I call it "change for a change." In this instance, it would require simply relaxing your breathing and the tightness in your chest or elsewhere in your body, and taking your *spotlight of awareness* from your thoughts and your gremlin's chatter to your visual field and beginning to *simply notice* the person in front of you.

BREATHE, DAMMIT, BREATHE

As I mentioned in the interview conducted by Doug Rucker, your breathing is both a barometer and a regulator of your experience. It is a barometer in that if you attend to it, it will tell you when you are in the beginning stages of making yourself uptight or making yourself anxious. When you become anxious, your breathing becomes shallow. Your awareness becomes concentrated in your mind rather than in your body and sensory receptors. The mind begins trying to find a solution to whatever circumstances have inspired your anxiety. But the mind is limited by its Hypnotic Pre-Convictions.

Meanwhile, your gremlin, the monster of your mind, seizes the opportunity. He'll quickly rustle and rummage through old files in the warehouse of your mind, seeking the perfect regret, resentment, put-down, catastrophic expectation, or combination of them all. Whatever he selects will be precisely suited to your unique vulnerabilities. Then he'll drop them into the foreground of your awareness, contaminating whatever has occurred with negative past experiences and fears about the future.

Thinking and feeling are both noble activities, and a balance between them is essential for your fulfillment, pleasure, and productivity. But when you cramp your breathing and get locked in your mind, you block feelings and limit your ability to sense and fully experience the world around you. You block the innate problem-solving abilities of the Natural You, the essence of which is your Heart.

Analysis is sometimes important and has its place in controlled doses, but too much time spent in analysis, fantasy, and memory can cause you to miss this life as it is being gifted to you right here and right now, and it can make you anxious and fretful. Too much time in thought can result in your spending an unhealthy portion of your life in your mind instead of in the world or in touch with your Heart.

While your mind, at times, is a humdinger of a gift, it's important to remind yourself that it belongs to you. As I suggested earlier, it's like a bank account, and it needs to be managed. It belongs to you—you don't belong to it. It's a bank account of ideas—HPCs—and it relates them to one another to make meaning. If you use what it contains with proper care and discrimination, it can be one of your best resources. It can help you get where you are going. But don't let it drive. (The Natural You, fueled by your Heart, has a better feel for the road—and for the vehicle.)

Proper breathing will help the Natural You maintain an efficient balance between your use of your mind and your use of your natural senses. Your awareness of your breathing is a remarkably efficient tool for monitoring how well you are doing the job of remaining cool, calm, collected, content, and in touch with your Heart.

Your breathing is also a regulator in that by modifying your shallow breathing and beginning to take in all the air you want and to exhale fully, you will eliminate the physical manifestation of unwanted tension and reconnect with your Heart.

Where you place yourself on the imaginary continuum, situation to situation, is your choice and your responsibility.

76

Here's why it matters. The degree of satisfaction and fullness of experience you'll enjoy in your life is tied to the quality of contact you provide yourself. When you place yourself at the uptight end of your imaginary continuum, you are unavailable to make a full Connection. Your level of contact is compromised. Your Connection with your Heart is less than it might be. It is impossible to be two places at once. Mired in your mind and enmeshed with your gremlin's catastrophic expectations, be they conscious or unconscious, you are unavailable for a rich Connection with your Heart or the world. At these times, the foreground of your experience is your fears, regrets, or Hypnotic Pre-Convictions. You are caught up in your mind and unavailable to make contact with the real world. Your Heart misses the experience.

"Uptight" is a literal term. When your breathing becomes shallow, as it does when you scare yourself or start fretting, you've cut off your wonderful sensory receptors. Instead of using your eyes for what they are intended—that is, to see—you give them away and are "up" in your head worrying about how you are being seen. Your awareness is stuck in the world of mind. You're viewing the world through a veil of concepts and HPCs—and remember, that veil is just a delicately woven net. In these moments, your attention is up in your mind and your body is tight. You are "Up Tight."

When you are uptight you are only partially, if at all, able to connect with anything but your gremlin. Your energy may become tied up in a duality, an encounter between you and your gremlin. By the same token, when you are feeling centered and clear—whole—your energy flows freely and is available to go toward the world, to love, to create, to fight, or to simply "be."

In my work with couples and families and businesses, I'm often struck by how little genuine contact people make with one another, even when their level of contentment and/or their livelihood is dependent on their mutual efforts. If I am to gain benefit from my relationship with you, I have to experience you and allow you to experience me. I have to focus my senses on you and, for the moment, be free enough of my own matters of mind to attend to you. And I must give you the opportunity to see and hear me and my thoughts and reactions by taking care to pay attention to myself, and to communicate to you my experience of my own thoughts and feelings regarding whatever matter is at hand.

The quality of your contact with other human beings hinges on a clear Intention to Connect. It's a choice you and I make in each and every moment, consciously or unconsciously, randomly or with concentrated conviction.

We're about to discuss a practical method for making a strong interpersonal connection with a fellow human. Before doing so, I'd like to ask that you have a clear Intention to Connect with what follows. If that means taking a break for a few moments, or until tomorrow, I hope you'll do so. I'm not going anywhere, and neither will your mind, your gremlin, or your Heart. Gremlin-taming is a lifelong process at which you're going to continually improve—so there's no rush.

PEELING THE ONION

Want to fully connect via a conversation? Want to really experience someone in your Heart and have that person experience you? Play with this option. Once you get this skill down, you'll never have to be uptight in an interpersonal encounter. I call it Peeling the Onion. In brief, here's the system:

Simply Notice
Describe
Hush
Breathe
Listen

I really want to come up with an acronym for you, but I'm not thinking too quickly on my feet today, and I have a publisher's deadline staring me in the face. How's this? SNDHBL (pronounced snidabul). Say it three times now, and teach it to someone later today. Then you'll have it down pat. When you use the acronym, you will be snidabuling. Use it often, and you will be a snidabulite.

Basically, you're going to vividly, using simple sentences, describe your current experience to another person. You'll then hush and breathe and listen, and before long, a new layer of your experience will emerge. Then, if you like, you can again describe it, hush, breathe, and listen. You are, after all, an authority on your experience as it is unfolding for you. You are living it. So you can be completely confident that if you describe your experience simply and accurately, you are being truthful and authentic.

Begin by *simply noticing* what's true for you in the moment. What you're thinking, perhaps, or what you're feeling in your body, something you're imagining or remembering, something you're observing in your immediate surroundings— something about the person with whom you're conversing, or something about your relationship to them.

Describe what you are noticing. In other words, report your experience *succinctly, accurately, and simply.* You may or may not choose to use the words "I'm noticing that . . ." or "I'm aware of . . ." but think them. Again, make your description succinct, accurate, and simple. You are living your experience as it is unfolding for you. You are the ultimate authority on your present experience. No one knows it better than you. So simply describe it in simple sentences in the same way you might describe a beautiful scene or a work of art. Use accurate semantics, remembering that there is a difference in what you know for sure and what you imagine. There is a difference, too, in what you feel and what you think. Thoughts occur in your head. Feelings are physical sensations that occur in your body.

A WORD ABOUT RESPONSIBLE SEMANTICS

Responsible semantics are clear and simple. Responsible semantics don't rely on verbal crutches, such as "Know what I mean?" or "Wouldn't you agree?" or "If you will" or "Is this making sense?"

"Know what I mean?" and "Is this making sense?" are courteous inquiries if you feel you are accurately expressing yourself and simply wondering if you're being understood. Used excessively, however, these phrases may imply that you don't know what you want to say or that you are too inarticulate to express it. If you don't know whether or not what you're saying makes sense, perhaps you'd be best served to get some clarity regarding what you want to say. Then say it, using simple language and, where possible, simple sentences. Step up to the plate.

Responsible semantics are accurate semantics. Responsible semantics are a means of leaping out from behind your act and showing up in the present moment. They place you smack-dab in the middle of your current Here and Now existence instead of a half step behind it. Again, the quality of the contact you make hinges on a clear Intention to Connect. In interpersonal relationships, responsible semantics contribute to a quality connection.

Responsible semantics put you in touch with your ability to choose how to respond to any situation as well as to any internal impulse, thought, feeling, fantasy, or memory.

They enhance your *Response Ability*.

Drop "need" when you really mean "want." Drop "can't"

when you mean "won't," "don't want to," or "choose not to." Steer away from "should" and "ought" (often, "should" and "ought" imply a lack of choice and free will).

Consider changing "I should" to "I choose to" or "I choose not to." Take responsibility for your choices. Live the truth of who you are. It feels good.

Attend to impersonal "we's," "they's," and "you's," too. Unless you were on the playing field, saying "We beat the Yankees" is stretching it, donchathink?

Okay, okay. I take it back, sort of. Having read the above, Leti, my loving, unrelenting, uncompromising, no-hype wife, just reminded me of something. According to her, when the University of California at Santa Cruz men's volleyball team (the "Banana Slugs" for whom our son is the head coach) got into the Division III final four, I high-fived Leti and bellowed, "We did it!"

Hey, I'm only human—but you get my drift.

And be careful with "it." Often, "it" fits. But sometimes "it" can be replaced with "I" or "you"—drawing you and whomever you're conversing with right into the middle of the current moment and in contact with each other. "It" can also keep you from giving and getting credit where credit is due.

Hearing the doorbell, Leti opened the front door. There before her were two youngsters decked out in their Cub Scout uniforms. One was holding a piece of paper, and the other held sample boxes of candy. The boys looked briefly at Leti as she greeted them, then at each other. The one holding the piece of paper began reading in a barely audible voice. The essence of his script was that they were Cub Scouts from pack so-and-so, and that they were selling candy to raise money for something, and would Leti like to buy some. Leti said, "I believe I'd like four boxes of peanut brittle," at which point the little reader got quite wide-eyed, looked at his friend, and blurted out, "*It* worked!"

Steer away from "why" questions, too. Often recipients of "why" questions hear "defend yourself," and they, of course, behave defensively. One illusion perpetuated by your gremlin after someone has wronged or disappointed you is this: if you understand "why," you will feel peace and harmony. Watch it, or your gremlin may lead you into that cerebral house of mirrors we discussed earlier. There are an infinite number of answers to some "why" questions, none of which is complete. Where whys are concerned, every answer opens the door to another "why" question.

Why he or she had an affair, flew the coop, or ratted on you may be hard to understand completely, but the bottom line is "because he or she wanted to." The gremlin myth at play here is this: "If I *think* about this enough, I will *figure out* why he or she did this to me, and then I will be at peace again." It's a lie. You'll be at peace again when, and only when, you take your awareness out of the house of mirrors.

Behind most questions, "why" questions included, is a statement. Consider asking yourself, "What is the statement behind my question?" What is my experience in relation to this other human before me at this very moment? How do I feel about him or her or about what he or she did? And what do I think about it?" Do a snidabul:

Simply Notice

Describe

Hush

Breathe

Listen

Think in terms of clearing your system—getting yourself feeling good again. If you imagine that in order for you to feel at peace you must receive a particular response from someone else, you're giving that person an inordinate amount of power over you and your level of contentment. And what if he or she doesn't cooperate? Are you committed to staying unhappy?

When you express yourself, match your voice and facial expression to what you're feeling on the inside, and describe what you're feeling accurately. Then, hush, breathe, and listen. Allow your awareness to drift back and forth between your breathing and the person with whom you are in conversation. This is not the time to be uptight—in your head thinking of what you want to say next. During the next few breaths' worth of time, the other person may very likely say something. If so, allow that person's words to come in, take another breath before responding, and then repeat the sequence.

Simply Notice

Describe

Hush

Breathe

Listen

Here are a few examples of clear and simple responsible semantics at play:

"I see your furrowed brow, and my guess is you're angry or worried."

"You are beautiful."

"I feel so sad."

"I'm noticing I want you to appreciate me."

"I'd like to throttle you."

"Leave me alone."

"I'm really enjoying your company."

"I don't want to."

"I like you."

"Yes."

"No."

If after you report your experience, the other person doesn't choose to say anything, you might end the conversation, or simply repeat the sequence again. Each time, before repeating the sequence of *simply noticing*, describing, hushing, breathing, and listening, you may wish to think these words: "Now what I'm aware of is . . ." It is very much like peeling an onion. Having lived your experience fully by noticing it and describing it, you will notice a new personal experience emerging within you—I guarantee you. Simply notice it, describe it in simple sentences, hush, breathe, and listen.

Remember, you are an expert where your experience is concerned. You are living it. You know precisely what is going on within you, and all you have to do is notice it, describe it, and hush. Hushing is the hardest part for some people.

You needn't overexplain. Friends and foes alike are smarter than we sometimes give them credit for. If your Intention is to Connect, and you have taken the time to notice your experience and to describe it simply and accurately, using responsible semantics, and if you've then hushed, breathed, and listened, you can leave the encounter knowing that you did your part. You showed up. You lived the truth of who you are. You gave the gift of you, and you were prepared to receive the gift of the other person. That is that, and that is plenty. What other people do with the gift is up to them. They can say thanks, give you a hug, run away screaming, or blow you a big raspberry. That's their choice. Your part is to do a good you.

Encounters like these are unpredictable. That's probably why expressing to others your thoughts and feelings, especially those about them, has been called taking a risk. When you express what is true for you about another person, you don't know if you're going to get roses or rotten tomatoes, especially if what you are revealing is more confrontational than complimentary. So why do it? It's exciting, that's why, and the possibilities it opens up can knock your socks off. It gives others the opportunity to know and like you rather than just to applaud or reject your act, and it gives you at least a shot at intimacy. It opens up the possibility of love, and often it feels terrific—like coming out of a dark hiding place, a place where you are safe but bored. It's a way of popping out from behind your act (pleasant though your act may be), landing on your feet in front of another breathing, feeling human being, and saying, "I'm me, and I'm here. Who and where are you?" It gives others a chance to know you, and it invites them to come out and frolic and cavort with you.

Over the past several years, one client after another has

85

bombarded me with reams of reasons why this sort of open display of selfhood is dangerous, if not downright foolhardy. I'll admit maybe sometimes it is, but most of the objections I've heard don't hold water.

One client finally got my drift and made an admirable, gutsy, perhaps even overzealous run at unabashedly putting himself "out there" by giving a woman he adored, but had dated for only two months, a beautiful and quite pricey oil painting she had admired at a recent gallery opening they had attended. While this gentleman is well heeled, he is not rolling in dough, nor is he weak minded. But he is loving, and he knows himself well enough to know that he derives great pleasure from giving. He described to me in detail how much he enjoyed planning the purchase and picturing the reaction of the lovely lady of his dreams. When he surprised her with the painting, she stammered and stuttered and said she didn't know if she should keep it. He just kept looking at her, beaming with glee at the pleasure of giving it to her and the excitement inherent in the unpredictability of the moment. Then it occurred to him that she wanted him to resolve her discomfort by insisting that she keep the painting or return it to him. But this man is a clear thinker. He knows where he ends and others begin—that miraculous sheath known as his skin. He just kept smiling and said something like this: "Oh, that's up to you. That's your part. My part was to give it to you."

She loved the painting (and, as it turned out, him as well), and she kept both. In the process they both learned something about responsibility, which is really no more than "response ability." You can greatly enhance your ability to truly connect with clarity and simplicity by at least strongly considering giving honest, open expression to your thoughts and feelings and letting others select and take responsibility for their responses to you. To not consider the potential consequences of your actions would, of course, be less than wise, but remember: catastrophic expectations, like dreams of glory, all occur in a fantastic field of make-believe. If your gremlin has you convinced that the field is filled with land mines, you are likely to freeze in one spot and forget that although life, sure enough, is one damn thing after another, it does not have to be the same damn thing over and over again.

I'm not big on rules, especially rules for something as ever-evolving as life on planet earth, and I would be the last one to tell you to always be open, or to always be closed, when you're wondering whether to express your thoughts and feelings about others. The key is that you have a choice. But before choosing to play it safe time after time by keeping your feelings and opinions to yourself, or being oh-so-cautious about how you express them, at least consider the potential for pleasure and excitement you might get if you *simply notice*, describe, hush, breathe, and listen.

ABOUT EYES AND EARS

In order to Connect with another human being and really give your Heart an experience of that person, it's important that you bring your attention to your own breathing for a few breaths, taking in all the air you want and exhaling fully. Breathe comfortably. Now take your *spotlight of awareness* and cast it on the other person. See her. This is different from looking at her. See her. Provide your Heart with an experience. This is what your eyes are intended for—to see with. See her. Peruse. You need not be shy about seeing. You have eyes—they are a gift to be used. Don't stare. Just relax and use your eyes to notice in the same way you do when you're watching a television program you're really enjoying, but in which you are not invested in the outcome.

And hear her. Let your Heart enjoy her voice. Listen as you would to some good music, or as I did to Big Jon and Sparkie on the radio. (Then, again, up your nose with a rubber hose, Big Jon. A puppet, for God's sake! Tear a guy's heart out, *woodya*? You shouldn't have taken the show on the road, Big Jon.)

Okay, a quick word about unfinished business. Unfinished

business can divert your attention and foul up your Intention and your Connection, the way it just did mine and yours. I left you, went into the warehouse of my mind, and got entangled with old stuff. Okay, I'm back now. Unfinished business can blow the deal. It will contaminate any relationship—unless, of course, you have a clear Intention to Connect. In which case, you can peel the onion and practice our system: *Simply notice, describe, hush, breathe, listen.*

He's late for the third time in your passionate three-week romance. You feel ripped off, disrespected, disappointed, and angry. If you're a seasoned gremlin-tamer, you run through "What's So? So What? So What? And What Now?"

What's so?

The son of a bitch is late again. I'm pissed.

So what?

I'm imagining he doesn't respect me, the way Dad didn't respect Mom. I'm also imagining he'll soon be getting out of the relationship and I'll feel abandoned, just as I did after Mom and Dad divorced.

So what?

I'll be alone forever and die a bag lady. That's ridiculous.

What now?

I'm going to tell him how I feel.

You don't rehearse. When he arrives, you *simply notice* your experience, describe it succinctly, hush, breathe, and listen. You are in touch with your breathing, and you intend to use your eyes and ears as we discussed, having processed through what's so, so what, so what, and what now. You've separated out the Hypnotic Pre-Conviction regarding Daddy from the inconsiderate slug standing before you.

There is no rage in you, just authentic anger and disappointment. You feel centered and clear. Your voice and facial expression match perfectly what you are feeling on the inside. Your words are something like these:

"I'm disappointed and angry, Duke. I really like you, and what's also true is I'm not okay with agreements being broken. If you say you're going to do something, I would appreciate you doing it."

You're aware of your breathing. You continue to take in all the air you want and to exhale fully, breathing at a natural, comfortable pace. Your gaze is steady. You're looking him in the eye, but you're not staring. You don't repeat yourself, and you don't explain or justify. Your Heart is receiving the experience of you being you. So is Duke's.

Remember, your Intention is to Connect. The quality of your Connection to whatever you are attending to in any given moment is the determinant of the level of vibrancy you will experience. Creating a rewarding relationship with a fellow human, a creative endeavor, a business venture, or anything else requires a clear Intention to make a solid Connection. Your Intention is to Connect—to give a gift to your Heart.

CONNECT WITH EACH STEP

Clinton was a big kid. He moved to Lubbock, Texas, from Minneapolis in 1959 when he was fifteen, and that's when I met him. We became fast friends, and a year later we both made our high school varsity football team by the skin of our teeth. We were sophomores then, and we didn't get much game time, so during games we spent a lot of time on the bench. After making sure none of the other players or coaches were looking, we scooped handfuls of dirt from the ground and rubbed them into our pants. We knew that after the game, the cheerleaders and other "poplar" girls would come down on the field, and we didn't want to be seen as the fresh-as-daisy greenhorns we were. We wanted them to love us. Our motivation was not holy. I don't want to imply that Clinton and I were no more than uncouth hunks of carnal impulse, but we were. We had desires, and we felt sure that pep rallies and being on the varsity football team could play a role in their fulfillment. Pep rallies took place in the gym. Debby Darby was our head cheerleader.

Debby had a winning smile and lovely legs. After Debby had the student body torqued up, stomping on the bleachers, whooping and hollering, the band—that is, the Plainsmen Band, the best band in the land—would burst into our fight song: "On you mighty Plainsmen, show them . . ." The crowd would go wild. Hell, it was all teenagers. Picture it—two-year-olds in big bodies that were changing inside and out fast. Strained pituitaries, flushing testosterone, warbling vocal cords, and no sense of reason; a mix of teen spirit and carnal confusion, resulting in a screaming, whooping, wild-haired frenzy, which, if misunderstood, would upset the less than warlike.

While Debby Darby was getting the crowd wired and ready, Clinton and I were outside, lining up with the rest of the varsity football players to stroll in two by two, flex-jawed and determined. We made our entrance only after the crowd, wrought up and backed by the band, was belting out these words from the fight song: "Hail to you our heroes; let us give a rousing cheer: Rah! Rah! Rah!" It was great.

We walked in through a side door at one end of the gym, and in a long double line strolled down one side of the gym floor in front of the crowd. We made our way to a set of special chairs set off by red and blue streamers.

Clinton and I had a pact to walk in each time together, and we had an ironclad agreement to take turns being the lucky one who got to be closest, and therefore most visible, to the crowd. It was good that our season consisted of ten games and therefore ten pep rallies rather than some odd number, because who would get more "near the crowd" entrances was far too emotional an issue to have been settled peacefully.

The side perks of being on the varsity football team in Texas in 1959 were glory, an acceptable adolescent identity, and eventually a letter jacket. But these were simply accoutrements to Clinton and me. Our shared desire was simply to be seen and adored so that we could each, ultimately, get to stroll down the hall with, if not Debby Darby, at least some other frosty-haired cheerleader on our arm, or better yet, fate willing, take her to the Circle Drive-In Theatre (our local passion pit).

One day, despite our best efforts, Clinton's Intention got clear. Instead of focusing on the possibility of love and lust in the future, he focused on Connecting with the next step to getting there.

It was on a Tuesday afternoon full-pads practice, and we were doing a drill called one on one. The team formed a circle. Then, Coach Duval, our head coach, picked two men (he called us men) to face off in the center. The two cocks got in their stances, beak to beak, and at the coach's whistle tried to tear each other apart. Hitting with fists was not allowed (not to mention stupid, given the helmets and gear we were wearing), but some did it anyway. It was a tense situation if you let your ego get involved, and I assure you that we, to a "man," had our egos involved. That day, Clinton went against Bubba Belew.

Texas high school football in the late fifties was a big deal, as was Bubba Belew. Bubba Belew was a senior, and in that time, in that day, in that community, he was an icon. Bubba Belew was the biggest, baddest, crudest, cruelest, brownest-toothed, lowest-rent human I had ever met. Clinton and I worshipped the ground he walked on.

Coach Duval bellowed, "Belew!" and Bubba shuffled his 265-pound body to the circle's center, his arms dangling damned near to his knees. He had snot on his face mask. The

91

coach eyed the boys in the circle, looking for at least a semi-worthy challenger for his prize galoot. Resigned to the collective mediocrity of the male mammals circled about him, he finally pointed at Clinton and mumbled, "Clinton, get out here." Clinton was a third-string nobody in Coach Duval's eyes, but at least he was large. Clinton hustled out. The rest of us breathed a sigh of relief.

I knew the coaches wouldn't let Bubba Belew kill Clinton, but I hoped Clinton wouldn't get hurt so badly he'd cry. It wouldn't be cool, the word would spread, and hell, he and I *did* hang out together.

Clinton had taken a lot of kidding since he had moved down from Minnesota. He talked differently from the rest of us, and he was overweight. I don't think Bubba Belew even knew his name, and more than once Bubba and his stud football senior cronies had called Clinton a fat Yankee. When Clinton hunkered down into his stance in the middle of the circle to face Bubba, Bubba guffawed and spat out, "I'm gonna bust a fat Yankee's butt." And he did.

Coach yelled, "Set! Hike!" and Bubba busted Clinton good. The clash of helmets and pads and bones was loud and unpleasant, and a few seconds later when Coach Duval blew the whistle again and the action stopped, Clinton's nose was bleeding big-time. Bubba's intention had been to knock the hell out of Clinton. Clinton's intention had been to get out alive and avoid making a fool of himself.

But the taste of one's own blood has a strange effect on teenage boys. It's a drug. To a young man, blood announces the arrival of stark reality, and when it's one's own, it trumpets in a clarity of purpose, be it kill or be killed, or head for the hills *now*. For Clinton, the former was true. His transformation was evident to all who witnessed it. Clumsy and unsure seconds before, he now looked primitive and strong. Clinton's lips were quivering with rage, and the area surrounding them was pure white. Blood still streamed from his nose.

Bubba turned to take his place back in the circle of admirers. The trainer offered Clinton a towel for his nose. You could have heard a muscle twitch in the seconds after Clinton refused the towel, pushed the trainer's hand away, and growled through gritted teeth, "Get your ass back out here, Bubba."

Bubba Belew stopped in his tracks and in mid-"yuk," then slowly turned and looked at Clinton in slack-jawed disbelief. He looked at Coach Duval, who, with a quick motion of his head, indicated to Bubba that he should get back out there. Clinton appeared to grow three or four inches and to be breathing determination. Light shot out of his eyes, and he looked hard and powerful. His rage was evident.

Clinton was not thinking about Debby Darby or any other cheerleader. His heart, his mind, and his body were set on one Intention with which he was fully Connected: whipping

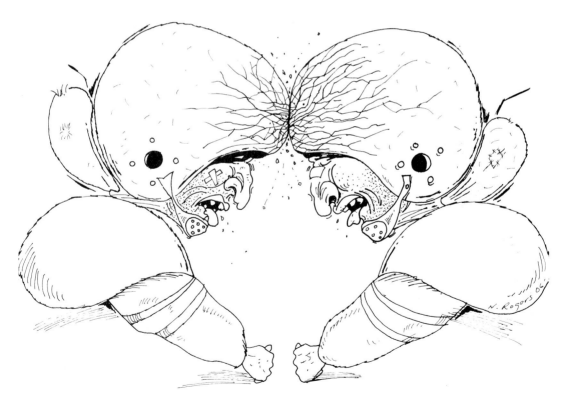

93

Bubba. And he did. Five times that day. Coach Duval kept them going at it. After all, Coach Duval's prize bull had gotten his dick knocked in the dirt by a kid he had treated all season as an also-ran. It didn't say much for his foresight as a coach, and I think he hoped Bubba would save face for both of them before the afternoon was out. Clinton bested them both.

Raw power guided by clarity of Intention and an uncompromised Connection is a hard combination to beat. One thing led to another. Clinton moved up to the starting lineup, and his date for the prom was Debby Darby.

Desire and Intention are different. Your desire may be to win the big game or her admiration, to climb Everest, or to surmount a slump. But Intention is a breath-to-breath activity. It has to do with choosing what you want to devote your attention to right Here, and right Now.

Certainly, it's a good idea to vividly picture the finished product—that is, to Connect with your desire. Where wellness and blue-ribbon performance are concerned, positive visualization is a worthwhile tool, as is supported by a wealth of data. But it's not enough. It's important to know where you are, where you want to be, and the precise stages leading from point A to point B. From my experience, more often than not, what separates getting there from going nowhere is a willingness to let your desire drift into the background of your experience long enough to let you Connect with the next small step leading from point A to point B, with the same enthusiasm and quality with which you first envisioned the desire. Give your Heart the gift of each step, and involve your Heart in the process of taking the step. In other words, achievement requires that your Intention be to fully and completely Connect with the next step toward fulfilling your desire.

An all-out Connection engenders a full-bodied experience. It doesn't always result in jump-up-and-down elation, and it's not always a pleasurable experience. It can even result in heart-throbbing terror or trepidation, even pain. (This morning I connected fully, or at least my shin did, with the corner of a coffee table I had managed to skirt past unharmed hundreds of times.) But with few exceptions, an Intentional Connection, be it with a thought, a human, a critter, a project, a fantasy, a memory, or Mother Nature, beats the hell out of the dead zone.

Combine a clear Intention with a clear choice to make a strong Connection predicated on Respect (for the fact that these are precious moments of your own life passing by), and phrases like "taking control of your life" start to make sense.

Chapter 15

Respect

After watching Texas Tech roust the University of Texas on our new TV set, Leti asked me a question. A damn good question. It made me proud to know her. Nibbling a Frito, she mused, "What's a draw play?"

"God love you, Leti," I thought. "Lord, thank you for coupling me with a worthy soul with sensible concerns." When the student is ready, the teacher will appear. I appeared.

I began as Professor Carson, stately and wise. I stood slowly, confidently gesturing with my right hand. I think my words were "It's like this . . ." My deft delivery failed briefly at this point. Where would I start? Leti had no real knowledge base. She lacked the theoretical underpinnings necessary to fully grasp the details, much less the nuance, of what was about to come her way. We would have to start with the basics.

Leti stayed with me through most of the essential elements of the game—hundred-yard field, end zones, four downs, turnovers, etc. And she seemed genuinely interested as I moved into the strategy behind passing on third down. She started looking a little bored when I detailed the interplay between the line and the backfield, and her eyes glazed slightly when I got into the difference between pass blocking and firing out for a running play. But this may have had to do with the fact that I was in an interior lineman's stance at the time. It affected my breathing and my voice, and it diluted the potency of my delivery. When I assumed the quarterback over "imaginary" center position to begin the answer to her original question about the draw play, she chomped down on another Frito and asked me what I thought we should do about dinner.

In a conversation with another person, it shows Respect to take into account what his or her current experience is, since, as my dad used to say, "you ain't the only pebble on the beach." It's helpful not to get so caught up in your own wit and wisdom that you forget to *simply notice* the other humans involved.

PROCESS AND CONTENT

Clear, respectful communication is an artful thing. It requires at least two folks, each a sender and a receiver of messages composed of an infinite number of components, including, but not limited to, words, voice tones, body postures, facial expressions, spatial relationships, tempo, cadence, desires, fantasies, historical baggage, protective maneuvers, and continuous choices. Two fundamental components are always at play: process and content. The content is the subject matter, that is, what's being discussed. The process is how and how well the information is being sent and received.

In the case of you and me at this moment, the *content* is "the difference between content and process." *Process* speaks to the quality of the relationship you and I are having—how strong our Intention is, how rich our Connection with each other is, the degree of Respect we have for what we're doing together, the care we've taken to create an Environment suited to what we're doing, how Authentic I'm willing to be with you, and how open you are to letting go of your HPCs *about* what

I'm saying in order to have your own Authentic experience of what I *am* saying. If we can both honestly say we're doing our part using I CREATE, we will have done all in our power to create a context for a richly rewarding Experience together.

Given that communication is a two-way endeavor, it makes sense to occasionally check with each other as to how well the process is going. It shows Respect.

So, I'd like to ask you, "How's it going?" I'd really like to ask if there's anything I can do to make our time together more pleasurable and meaningful, but given that I'm over here in a different time and space from yours, I couldn't do much with the information. So let me ask you the same question: "Anything you can do to make our time more pleasurable and meaningful? Changing the thermostat, maybe? A cup of tea? A deep breath? A big stretch? A run around the block? A snooze?" If so, not a problem. I'll be right here at your service when you choose to reengage.

In almost four decades of working with families and organizations toward creating rewarding relationships, I've noticed a few patterns in the ways people demonstrate a lack of Respect for one another. Some are overt, some are covert. Among them are these:

Overexplaining

This tactic is often based on the illusion that more is better. Typically, people who overexplain their point of view also tend to repeat themselves, subliminally giving the message that the person they are talking with is too shallow to quickly grasp the information being imparted.

As we discussed in our "peeling the onion" section, a few clear, simple, descriptive sentences, followed by a few easy breaths and an open mind are far more valuable than lengthy pontification. Besides, as you as the sender keep talking, you let the receiver off the hook. You set up a dynamic in which you take excessive responsibility for being understood. This may lessen the other party's effort to really mull over what you're saying. Ever been an adolescent, or a parent of one? Lecture does not work.

Talking about someone instead of talking to him or her
Known in common parlance as gossip, this behavior wreaks havoc with interpersonal relationships of every ilk, including friendship, romance, and business.

Every organization and family is no more than a network of people—souls wrapped in bodies peering out at one another. To describe our thoughts and feelings to one another, using simple sentences and respectful, responsible semantics, need not be nearly as threatening as we sometimes imagine. If you can say something about someone, you probably could say it to him or her and survive. Talking *about* someone as well as *to* that person is sometimes helpful, and often it's done out of caring. But talking about someone *instead of* talking directly *to* the person creates a breeding ground for unfinished business and bad energy. Healthy human systems are dynamic, not static. They change constantly, and the change agent is feedback from the human beings involved in the system. If the system has no new input, it will degrade, going into a state of entropy. Simply put, it will get unbearably dull.

Remember, your gremlin loves the status quo because he knows it inevitably leads to degradation. He wants you trapped in your mind, reliving your HPCs about life instead of living in your life. If that doesn't *dull* you out, he'll try to *freak* you out by taunting you with catastrophic fears in an attempt to help you avoid taking the risk to step out from your disguise. That's his job. As for his disguises, they take many forms. When he's taunting you, he's akin to a wild-eyed court jester with a bent toward sadism. Get stuck in the warehouse of your mind, engaged by your gremlin, and you are likely to get really anxious or enter the dead zone.

Rushing to share a parallel experience

So what if you've also been to Tahiti? Take the time to listen to what Lulu has to say about her trip there.

Interrupting

Sometimes I guess you've just got to, in order to get a word in edgewise or to indicate that you've gotta split, but all in all, interrupting is a bad idea. Saying "I don't mean to interrupt, but . . ." doesn't absolve you of your responsibility for your choice.

Habitual lateness

The fundamental message to those waiting for you is "I'm important. You're not important." Apology may help, as may elaborating on how much the folks you've kept waiting mean to you, but actions speak louder than words.

Not returning phone calls or responding to e-mails within twenty-four hours

Not acknowledging acts of kindness

Avoiding eye contact

When in conversation with someone, spend at least a portion of the time looking into the eyes of the person you're conversing with. You need not stare. A soft gaze is better, and it is natural to look away every few seconds.

Keep your breathing clear and relaxed, and find a natural rhythm between looking toward and looking away—between contact and withdrawal. Remember, your eyes are for seeing. Instead of giving your eyes away to others, and then worrying about how you're being seen, relax, and use your eyes to see them.

Mumbling

Fidgeting

Don't leave. We're not through when it comes to showing a lack of respect; there is an unlimited array of possibilities.

Jumping to conclusions

Sometimes we can be so locked in our preconceived notions about what others think and feel that we don't really listen to them. Bad idea. You'll have your time to reflect on and share your point of view after you've heard them. When it's your turn to listen, listen. Let go of rehearsing your response. Hear.

Being phony

Sorry—you're just as transparent as the rest of us.

Sarcasm

If this is the way you and your intimate others play, and it's done with no malice, good for you.

When sarcasm is an outgrowth or symptom of unfinished business, anger, or resentment, however, it is mightily dis-respectful. Ask yourself what you really want to say, and say it, using simple sentences and responsible semantics. *Simply notice*, describe, hush, breathe, and listen.

Doing more than one thing in any breath's worth of time

Get your Intention clear. Decide what, or whom, you want to attend to, and devote yourself to it or them. If you don't want to take the time to Connect with the person before you, say what's true:

"I really want to hear what you have to say, but not now. I'm late for the dentist. I'll call you later."

"I'm glad you're glad the Mavericks won. I don't want to talk about that anymore now."

To hold back the truth is a put-down to you and a put-down to the person with whom you are conversing. It suggests that

101

you're not entitled to your reality and that the other person is too weak to handle the truth.

Assuming that there is an unalterable truth and that you are the bearer of it

Mahatma Gandhi had more than one poignant comment on this theme: "The golden rule of conduct . . . is mutual toleration, seeing that we will never all think alike and we shall see Truth in fragments and from different angles of vision." (Actually, my favorite Gandhi quote is the one he issued when asked what he thought of Western civilization: "I think it would be a good idea.")

Huffing, puffing, and rolling of eyes

Inflection and intonation that implies that your comment could well end with "Stupid," even though you're not saying it

Spinning on one's heels, storming off, and slamming doors and/or cabinets

How about putting in your own two cents' worth, here? What disrespectful behaviors most get your goat? Jot down a few.

_____

_____

_____

Now put a check mark to the left of the one that bothers you the most.

Using a simple sentence or two or three, and responsible semantics, describe below how you feel and what you think when you witness that behavior in someone. Begin your first sentence with "I."

_____

_____

_____

Next time you encounter this behavior from someone, consider saying what you've just written, then hush, breathe, and listen. Doing so shows, and teaches, Respect.

Your gremlin loathes this unabashed showing up—so he'll no doubt taunt you with catastrophic expectations regarding your bold behavior:

"Don't rock the boat, Babycakes."
"What are you thinking? You could get us killed."
"You really don't have much to offer, Sugar Lips.
People will like you better if you just smile and nod."

Simply notice. Play with options. Be in process.

Respect yourself and others enough to live the truth of who you are in their presence.

But what if you don't respect the person, place, or thing with which you are connecting? Driving to work yesterday, I saw three similar but equally bizarre events. I saw three different people, two women and a man, in three separate cars, with their windows rolled about halfway up, their left arms protruding through the space between the top of the window and the top of the car door. Their fingers held cigarettes. Each of these people was going to a lot of trouble to smoke. I assume, therefore, that their desire to do so was a strong one. But the fact that they had their arms thrust out the window, probably to avoid having their clothes and the interior of their cars smell like cigarette smoke, revealed their mixed feelings about smoking. This sort of approach/avoidance attitude is present when we consider connecting with a person, place, or thing we don't fully respect.

If you're going to expend precious moments of your God-given life connecting with something or someone, for crying out loud, find a way to respect it or them and/or to respect the time you're spending—or consider not connecting. If you choose to smoke, smoke. Suck that poison down into your lungs, inhale with all your might, and blow it out with glee. Otherwise, why smoke? If you're not sure you want to be doing what you're doing, why the hell are you doing it?

I like and respect all my current clients. I admire their bravery and their creativity. We have a mutual Intention and a strong Connection, which results in a vibrancy and, simply put, a lot of good times for my Heart (and theirs). But there have been occasions in the past, and there may be in the future, when I find myself with someone whose persona I don't respect. Maybe our politics and/or our values are dramatically different. I notice, for example, that I usually don't immediately respect people who are not willing to take responsibility for their part in creating their own unhappiness.

But even if I find myself working with someone whose values I'm not wild about, what I do indeed respect is the fact that my time with them is composed of precious moments of my very own life.

I don't know how many breaths I'll get in this life, but I do know I'm not about to waste any of them. So, given that I've chosen to spend several breaths' worth of time in the presence of this other person, whether I initially respect that person's style of being or not, I most certainly am going to respect that the time I'm spending with him or her is my time. These are moments of *my* life. I'm not going to be less than fully engaged.

I am not about to cheat myself or my Heart out of the experience or the opportunity to connect completely. I intend to be fully *in* the relationship. I *Intend* to devote all of myself to whomever I'm *Connecting* with during the time we are together.

Again, my *Intention* is to *Connect* because I *Respect* each breath's worth of time as a gift I have been given, and I respect the opportunity to offer my Heart an experience.

An Intention to Connect with Respect comes into play not just in your relationships with people but in your relationships to projects, such as artistic endeavors, athletic objectives, or business ventures.

PLANNING AND DOING

When it comes to planning and doing, some folks are great at seeing the big picture—that is, forming a fantasy of how it could be—but have difficulty attending to details. This may work for you if you're rolling in dough, or if you are such a shining star that you can demand the time, devotion, and effort of top-notch detail people. For most of us, however, it's important to remember that dreaming comes easy, and that the chasm between big ideas and a high-quality finished product is deep and wide.

Often what separates a win from a washout is the willingness to focus not only on the end goal but, more important, on the willingness to relegate the end goal to your background of experience for a spell and to intentionally bring the next tiny step toward goal attainment into your foreground. Doing so means Respecting each small step. You won't take each step with quality if your Heart is not involved with it. Stay aware of the relationship between the step you're taking (tedious though it may be) and the fulfillment of your desire. It will help. Intention springs from desire, and the best desires spring from your Heart. Connection is the result of giving something—anything—your all: your very best effort. You aren't about to give yourself fully to anything if you don't *Respect* either what you're *Connecting* with or that the time and energy you're spending connecting with it is time and energy well spent.

Here's a simple formula for accomplishing or producing something worthwhile:

Know what you want to accomplish.

105

Write down the steps necessary to get it done.

Set a date for gracefully taking each step.

Be willing to change the dates without giving up the project.

Establish a clear Intention to Connect with Respect to each step.

Take the steps.

Dr. Jonas Salk, in the process of discovering the polio vaccine, conducted more than two hundred formal experiments. When asked by an interviewer how he felt about those two hundred failures, Dr. Salk pointed out to the interviewer that he couldn't identify with the word "failure." He explained that to him, each experiment was an important part of the trial-and-error process of accomplishing what he wanted to accomplish. He respected each step. Thank goodness Jonas stuck with it. Polio in its time was as great a threat as the AIDS virus is today, and thanks to his persistence, we've got polio under control.

As you and I try to influence our destiny we are sure, from time to time, to get so caught up in dreaming about our destination, or get so distracted from it, that we take an occasional fall. But while we're sprawled out there on the ground, let's pick something up—a piece of wisdom, maybe. Then let's pull ourselves upright, dust ourselves off, and move on with our project. To do so, simply remember that your Intention is to Connect with Respect to each step. Respect each step enough to let your Heart be involved with it.

Respect the relationship between your goal and each small step by creating steps that are manageable in size. If you try to build your bridge between where you are and where you're going with planks that are too weighty or unwieldy, setting them in place will appear to be such a struggle that you may avoid trying it.

By the same token, don't overdo on the detail work. It's

okay for your bridge to look spiffy, but if you get hung up chiseling and sanding each plank into a master woodcrafter's work of art, you may grow feeble before you get the bridge built and yourself across it. This may not be a bad way to spend time if it keeps you happy, but if you think you'll be even happier once it's built, you'll be better served to keep moving and to keep your focus.

Staying focused requires conscious Intention. I emphasized earlier that your awareness is a spotlight that you control. It is. But sometimes the props and players in your world may jump up and down, yell at you, or sing you a ditty and do a tap dance, trying to get you to shine your light on them instead of on the step you're Connecting with.

GET YOUR INTENTION CLEAR

You can't be in two places at once, so if your attention is split, simply get your Intention clear as to what you want to Connect with, and Connect all-out.

You might consciously choose to change your Intention to what you want to attend to. You might choose to make what you've heretofore seen as a distraction the main event for a brief period of time. It's okay to put down the pen and paper and get into petting Sophie for a few moments, or let the bill paying go while you let your kid demonstrate her perfect cartwheel.

Keep your Intention clear. Consciously select where you want to focus your beam of awareness—how broadly and brightly, and for how long. Staying centered will help you stay focused, as will keeping your breathing clear and relaxed and connecting with it often. Remember, the idea is to gently control your *spotlight of awareness*, moment to moment and breath to breath. Your Heart is waiting. You are the locus of control. You decide, breath to breath, what you want to Connect with. Your *Intention* is to *Connect* with *Respect* for the breaths of time you are spending.

If it's your gremlin who's vying for your attention and you decide to engage with him for a time-limited period, get fully into doing so. You may not respect your gremlin, but definitely respect the precious moments of your life you're choosing to devote to him. Remember, buried in his chatter might be a tidbit or two you can use. So give the information at least a nod. Notice it. That's plenty. Remember, where "gremlinology" is concerned, a little thought is a lot.

Also remember that your gremlin is your gremlin by virtue of his intention, not by virtue of the information he whispers in your ear or pounds you over the head with. Simply notice what he has to say. Consider it, briefly. It has whatever meaning you choose to give it. Notice it, and trust your Heart, the essence of the Natural You, to use what fits and to eliminate what doesn't.

Say you impulsively react to an associate's bungling of a project by snapping at her. You see her wince. As you walk away you enter the world of mind, where your gremlin, seizing the opportunity, attacks. "Now, you've done it, you stupid, inconsiderate moron. Can't you do anything right?" You *simply notice* that your breathing is shallow and that you're tensing your neck and shoulders. You *accentuate* the tension in your body and your gremlin's chatter, turning up the volume on what he has to say.

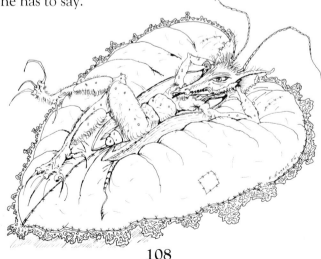

**"You're not only stupid; you're mean.
Have you no sense of diplomacy? How old are you—six?
No wonder no one likes you."**

You accentuate more. You intentionally make your breathing even more shallow. You tighten your neck and shoulder muscles more than before. You do so on purpose. You intentionally furrow your brow. You then get to choose.

You choose to modify your breathing; you relax, taking in all the air you want and exhaling fully. You relax your facial muscles and the tension in the rest of your body. You keep what you can use from your gremlin's chatter and eliminate the rest. You re-approach your colleague and describe what you're noticing. "I'm afraid I hurt your feelings, and I feel bad about it. I'm sorry I snapped at you." You then hush, breathe, and listen. She says, "Thank you. I appreciate your apology," or "I don't care what you think, Pea Brain. Go take a long walk on a short pier," giving you yet another glorious opportunity to practice taming your gremlin.

If your Intention is to fully Connect and you Respect the opportunity you're being given, it makes sense to attend to the Environment in which you Intend to form a Connection. That's where we'll turn our spotlight next.

Chapter 16

Environment

For two years after Eva died, a deep sadness permeated my soul. Eva was special to me. She was my friend and my mother and the last to die in her family of origin and mine (I miss my dad and brother as much). I loved Eva. I loved my mother. And I liked her and I respected her. I respect her to this day as much as any human I have ever known or heard about.

Eva was a unique blend of say-it-like-it-is wisdom, set-jawed determination, and unabashed love. Under circumstances that for many would have been damned near unbearable, she was tough as nails. She was a good soul, and I'm fortunate to have known her, much less to have called her Mother.

Eva's death, possibly because it called forth all the unfelt emotions from my dad's and my brother's deaths, demanded—absolutely demanded—that I feel the depth of sadness and love that comes with saying good-bye forever.

But my mind wasn't ready. It clung to ideas—ideas about who I am, how I mourn, how it all works, how it is. My mind, not for the first time, cheated me, imposing overlapping thought forms—*aboutisms*. Thoughts *about* how I felt—ideas *about* missing and mourning and longing—*about* sadness and regrets, *about* good-bye and *about* what now? For a while it cheated me out of my own experience of my own life. Eventually, with the help of the right day, time, and setting—the right Environment—my experience shifted.

I had been one of the keynote speakers at a beautiful three-day conference for personal coaches held in Herzliya, near Tel Aviv. The conference was sponsored by Coach Me, a training organization for life coaches and executive coaches, and it was the brainchild of Yoram Gordon and his lovely wife, Sunny Gordon-Bar, two of the most loving and grandest souls I've ever met. After the conference, Sunny and Yoram graciously arranged a three-day tour for three of the other speakers and me. They provided us with a superb guide, a driver, and a van large enough for all of us, including Sunny and Yoram. I enjoyed my traveling companions immensely, and the tour was a richly rewarding experience.

The third day of the tour was a chilly, drizzly morning. We spent several hours in Jerusalem, basking in the history of that ancient and timeless city. Then we visited the Western Wall.

The Western Wall is in the midst of the Old City. It is a section of the western supporting wall of the Temple Mount, which has remained intact since the destruction of the Second Jerusalem Temple in 70 CE. The Western Wall is the most sacred location in Jewish religious and national consciousness and tradition by virtue of its proximity to the Holy of Holies in the Temple.

In keeping with Orthodox practice, the exposed length of the wall has been cordoned into two sections—one for men and one for women. A low barrier forty or fifty feet from the wall keeps sightseers apart from the area reserved for prayer and religious ritual. Though most of those praying are ultra-Orthodox Hasidic Jews, any man, Jew or non-Jew, may enter the men's enclosure so long as he is wearing a head covering.

I was standing, talking with my traveling companions outside the barrier, but my Heart yearned to approach the wall. In order to do so, as I mentioned, custom dictated that I cover my head. Not realizing that cardboard head coverings were available, I borrowed a baseball cap from one of my traveling companions and walked beyond the barrier toward the wall. Standing before the wall, I felt compelled deep in my Heart to lay my right hand on it. My left hand followed and, within a few seconds, my forehead.

Often, such as when I meditate, I make every effort to open myself and surrender to the experience of the moment. Especially when I meditate, the last thing I want to do is contaminate my experience by imposing my ideas. But I've never had an experience of open, complete surrender like the one I had standing there with my hands and forehead resting on the wall. I felt completely open, and a simple, beautiful peace permeated my existence. I was an empty vessel in perfect bliss, simply waiting.

Each person on the planet has his or her very own unique feel. Call it energy or essence or whatever. It's what we most miss when they die. We may also miss their personality, the feel of their skin, and other aspects of their existence—those things that we talk about at the funeral. But it's that unique essence that was theirs that we most miss. There within me, I felt the essence of my father first and then my brother and then my mother. The experience lasted for three or four minutes. Tears and sobs came from a place within me so deep I didn't know it existed. I surrendered to the profoundly rich experience of loss. It was beautiful, and wrought with none of the anguish that had accompanied its confinement—my imprisonment—by my very own mind.

As I've emphasized throughout this book and in others, events occur around you, and you are a participant in some, but your experience of those events occurs within the boundary defined by your skin. I have often stated, "While it comes in handy to be able to manage your circumstances, it comes in even handier to be able to regulate your inner experience regardless of circumstances." Now that I've said that, the right configuration of props and players—that is, the right Environment—can certainly be a boon to any experience.

Your Environment includes everything from your Heart, on out. It includes how you feel in your body (your breathing, of course, and where you are on the imaginary continuum we discussed earlier); the physical setting in which you wish to form a Connection, including furniture, the spatial relationship between you and whatever or whomever you're choosing to connect with, temperature, kinesthetic and audiovisual factors; and the potential for distraction.

Do you and your lover really want to discuss the future of your relationship while drinking wine?

Is sleeping with the television on truly the best way to have a restful night's sleep?

Is the annual review of one of your key account managers really something you want to do over lunch or cocktails?

Maybe so. But it's definitely worth asking yourself how strong your *Intention* is. What kind of *Connection* do you really want to make? How much do you *Respect* the task at hand? And what sort of *Environment* is best suited to your Intention to fulfill your desire?

When someone contacts my office to make an appointment, my Intention is to form a rich Connection reflective of the Respect I have for the time we're going to spend together and for the opportunity we are being given. I want the Environment to be conducive to swiftly forming the deepest connection possible. But it's a weird set of circumstances. After all, on the surface the arrangement is pretty stilted.

Think of it: The motivation for people who contact me is that they are, in all likelihood, going through the toughest transition or roughest loss they've ever experienced. Though they've usually been referred by someone who's told them I can help, we first encounter one another as complete strangers.

113

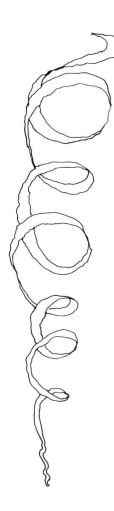

Our meetings typically are scheduled for forty-five minutes and occur only once every week or two. And they have to pay for our time together. What is more, I expect my clients to be more unguarded and honest with themselves than they have ever been in their entire lives, and to be so in my presence. Sounds awful, huh?

In reality, the process is typically graceful and abundant with good goings-on. By the end of our first session, the Connection almost always feels good to both of us, and we are well engaged in the task at hand. So, how does this happen? I CREATE.

My staff and I live I CREATE. We're greedy for experiences of the Heart. When I hired my assistant, Kim Harrison, it wasn't for her computer and typing skills (I kid Kim by telling her that when I hired her she typed thirty or forty words a minute, give or take a *minute*).

I offered Kim the job because I liked her immediately. I liked the way she related to me in our interviews. She was honest and forthright, her breathing was clear, her face was relaxed, and she seemed to be using her eyes to see instead of worrying about how she was being seen. She listened carefully, as reflected by her sincere questions and obvious curiosity. Her voice was pleasant, and she didn't hem and haw. She was nicely dressed. She was clearly professional in her demeanor, but this blended with her gentle good nature and sense of humor. When we discussed the many nuances and considerations of my work, she had many questions and listened intently to my answers. She really seemed to want to know. She Connected.

Whether a client's first contact with our office is via telephone, e-mail, or a face-to-face meeting, Kim is typically the person he or she first encounters. So you can easily comprehend why finding someone like Kim, who is clear-eyed, appreciates the nature of my work, and represents me accordingly in that first encounter, is so critical for me. She plays a key role in creating the Environment I want for all who enter my door.

Remember, where my clients are concerned, our *Intention* is to *Connect*. We *Respect* the opportunity we are being given, and we want every aspect of our clients' experience with us to reflect this. *Environment* is key. The office, the waiting room, and the room where I meet with clients are designed around our *Intention* to *Connect* with *Respect*.

I want the environment in which I work to reflect my fundamental tenets of service, among them this principle: "You, dear client, are responsible and capable." A sign in my office states, "We do not consider our service to be a medical treatment . . . If you think you are mentally or physically ill, see a medical professional."

We do not think of, or refer to, the consumers of our service as "patients." We see them as clients. To refer to my clients as patients would be patronizing, and I think it would subliminally give the message that they have an illness of some sort, which renders them incapable of maximum functioning. I rarely buy that this is the case. I refuse to collude with people in perpetuating the Hypnotic Pre-Conviction that they are less than fully capable or responsible. That's their gremlin's tactic, and when he berates, bashes, or whispers his ballyhoo about their limitations, my clients soon learn what to do. They *simply notice* (Chapter 3, revised edition of *Taming Your Gremlin*), *play with options* (Chapter 8, *Taming Your Gremlin*, r.e.), and *stay in process* (Chapter 11, *Taming Your Gremlin*, r.e.).

Confidentiality, too, is an important aspect of the *Environment* in which my clients and I do our work. What goes on in our sessions is kept completely confidential from my side. My clients, of course, have the option of discussing our sessions with others, but I ask that they not do so if they think this will dampen the unique and special nature of our relationship. I want our time together to feel like an escape from earth. I want to provide them with a time-out zone from day-to-day existence where there awaits a skilled ally, completely devoted to helping them enrich their breath-to-breath experience. All this contributes to an Environment suited to my Intention to Connect with Respect.

Our clients are given no forms to complete until the end of their first session with me. I want them Connecting with me, not a form. And while our intake form is thorough, it is streamlined and requires no more than twenty minutes to complete.

The room where I conduct sessions is quiet and comfortable and is set up exclusively to allow my clients and me to be at ease and to Connect with one another and the issues at hand, with no distractions. There is no table or desk between us, and my chair is on rollers so I can constantly adjust the space between us.

Though I'm definitely in charge of the process, the relationship between my clients and me is still somewhat collegial. It is a team effort, and each of my clients and I constitute a team. Over time, we become a stronger, more efficient team toward the accomplishment of our mutual desire—the enhancement of their existence. That is, more moments spent in the pleasure of being fully aware and fewer spent in the displeasure of being stuck in bad relationships, baffled, rudderless, spaced out, deadened, or in outright pain.

While most of my clients do indeed increase their overall level of contentment, eliminate Hypnotic Pre-Convictions, throw out destructive Habitual Behavior Patterns, work through dualities, change behaviors, and learn new skills, I don't "cure" them of anything. There is no cure for being human, and while for some it is a tough pill to swallow, none of us will ever be permanently deprived of the option of making ourselves completely miserable or of screwing up our lives.

Any person, any project, any endeavor you Intend to Connect with will bring you more satisfaction if you Respect it enough to give a little thought to the Environment in which you are forming the connection. I'm writing these words longhand, sitting in a library. I'm writing longhand because I like the feel of my pencil on my paper. I'm in this particular library because it's generally quiet, but not too quiet. There's just enough background noise. The lighting is superb: soft, but just right for what I'm doing. I like the temperature in here and that there is a floor-to-ceiling window to my left, which looks out on a large bed of ferns shaded by three oaks and a giant pecan tree. It's a perfect Environment for Connecting with Respect to the opportunity to be in communion with you. While my home and my office are both places where I love hanging out, and great environments for lots of what I enjoy, both have telephones and abundant reminders of other things that could use doing.

How's your Environment now? Is it suited to the strongest possible Connection between you and me? How strong is your Intention to Connect? Do you Respect the task at hand? Remember, your Environment contains everything from your Heart out, including how your body feels, your physical setting, your clothes, and of course your state of mind.

I'm honored that you're spending time Connecting with me. I am truly honored that from within the boundary defined by your skin you are choosing to peer out at these words. In there, at this moment, you will choose to read on or to stop. You would make this choice whether I mentioned it or not, and probably you would do so without consciously thinking about it. By mentioning it, however, I have brought it into your conscious mind, and now you must think about it. Notice that to do so requires energy and feels a little like work.

You can easily see how too much thinking can fry your circuits and manifest in symptoms such as ulcers, heart attacks, job burnout, car wrecks, substance abuse, and incoherent babbling. There is a difference between simply making a choice and *trying* to make a choice. There is a difference between effort and strain. Having and maintaining a clear Intention to Connect with Respect requires effort. It does not require strain.

What is your Intention at this moment? And what is your

inner experience? Are you relaxed and open, so that the meaning of these words can float in through your eyes down to your Heart? Are you distracted or restless? Confused, perhaps, or bored? Are you trapped in your mind, working hard to make meaning? If this is true, your gremlin may be on the scene. If he's gotten to you, your breathing might be shallow, and you may feel a sense of frustration and/or tension in your body. If this is so, either choose to focus on your gremlin's chatter for a brief period, perhaps even accentuating it as we discussed previously, or simply relax your breathing, focus on my words instead of on his chatter, and read on with a clear Intention to Connect with Respect in an Environment suited to making the best possible Connection. Or—take a break, and come back when you have a clear Intention to Connect. I'll be right here when you return.

Throughout this day, as you select, moment to moment, situation to situation, what or whom you want to connect with, give a little extra thought to the Environment in which you are attempting to make the Connection. If your Intention is to Connect with your spouse in order to discuss your finances, how about sitting facing each other in a quiet room with no distractions? Anytime you have a conversation with anybody, remember: your Intention is to Connect with Respect in an Environment suited to your Intention to Connect with Respect. Your Heart is waiting.

When you participate in the mainstream of people's consciousness day in and day out, as I do, you notice some interesting trends. One of them is that people have lofty expectations about lots of things. Interpersonal relationships, for instance; a good night's sleep; even life itself.

Let's stay with the sleep thing for a minute. It comes up in my office daily. A client of mine recently said he hadn't slept for two days. I asked him why in the world he wanted to sleep for two days. He didn't laugh.

Seriously, not only are some people hooked into the belief

that they should feel happy all the time, but get this one: A lot of people think something's wrong if they don't sleep through the night.

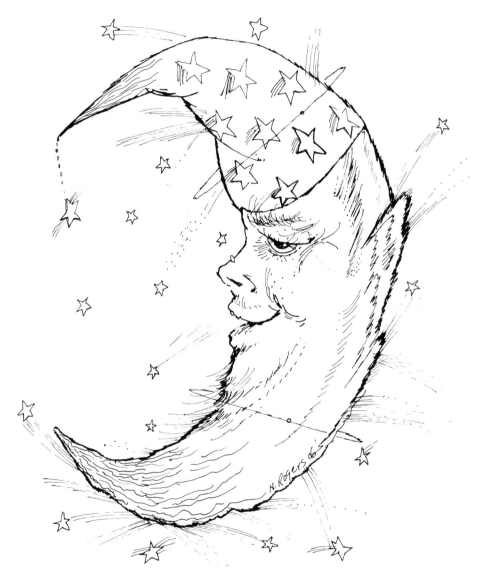

Now hear this! According to my informal survey, from what I hear in my office and what I hear from my friends and family, many people rarely sleep soundly and completely through the entire night. It's not uncommon for people to wake up one, two, or three times—some to pee, some to fret, some for no apparent reason. Don't let your gremlin make it a bigger deal than it is.

Now that I've said that, if your Intention is to get a good night's sleep, prepare for bedtime by fully Connecting with that Intention and Respect the steps involved in creating an Environment for doing so. Again, remember that your Environment is everything from your Heart out, including your body. You know the basics. Easy on the caffeine and sugar (including alcohol), no heavy meal or exercise near bedtime, perhaps a hot bath before hitting the hay, and some relaxing music as a way of winding down.

Remember, too, that your Environment includes your clothes. Whether you prefer fine lingerie, flannel pajamas, or your birthday suit, get comfortable. And of course your Environment includes the room in which you're going to sleep. Make it quiet, comfortable, dark, and at a temperature you feel good in. And for goodness' sake, take some care with your bed—suit it to your unique preferences, and use it only for sleep (and sex). This way, when you go to bed, your body and your brain will be conditioned to your Intention in doing so.

As for life itself—isn't it gift enough just to be alive and present? What an opportunity. Desire more? Wonderful. Go for it. Expect more? You set yourself up for a lot of disappointment.

There is a keen difference between desires and expectations. Your gremlin loves the latter. He'll keep them coming at you. Expectations are like cockroaches. No sooner do you get free of one batch than a whole new colony will invade—courtesy of the monster of your mind. Remember, your Environment includes everything from your Heart out, including your state of mind. Don't clutter your warehouse of the mind with expectations—or cockroaches.

Whether at any moment your Intention is to have a restful snooze, practice yoga, write a book, study, run around the block, negotiate a deal, or make love—give some thought and effort to designing an Environment worthy of your unabashed giving of yourself.

As for the *attire* aspect of creating a sensible Environment, here's a good guideline for almost any activity. Pick clothes that are comfortable enough to dance in. (Whether you ever go dancing is immaterial.)

Leti and I used to go dancing quite often at a wonderful honky-tonk in Dallas called the Longhorn Ballroom. It was practically an institution because it catered to people who truly liked to dance, rather than simply strut their stuff or try to pick up somebody. For the most part, it was an older crowd. I was often struck by how most of the patrons wore stylish country-western duds that were also soft and comfortable. Comfortable enough for dancing.

But one evening, Leti and I both noticed a young woman on the dance floor who looked miserable. She obviously was there to dance, as she and her date were on the dance floor constantly, but clearly her boots were way too small for her feet. To make matters worse, she must have greased her buttocks in order to slip into her jeans, which had to have been two to three sizes too small for her full frame. And she had her jeans tucked into her boots. I swear, if she had farted, she would have blown her boots off.

Remember, your Environment includes everything from your Heart out, including your body, your clothes, your spatial relationship between you and whatever or whomever you're connecting with, all that is immediately available to you via your senses, and of course your state of mind.

While you're practicing *simply noticing*, and having a clear *Intention* to *Connect* with *Respect* in every moment, and while you're asking yourself, "Gosh-a-rootie! What's the best *Environment* for doing so?" your mind sits like Jabba the Hutt and absorbs experiences. Your gremlin twists these experiences into movies about who you are and how the world works. Your mind is like a freakin' multiplex theater with an infinite number of movies playing. Some are realistic, but none are real. They may mimic reality, but they are not reality. Your mind is not innately evil; it simply needs to be seen for what it is. The monster of your mind, your gremlin, is akin to a carnival barker who entices you into the theater of the mind, then switches hats and ushers you into those movies that for you are most personally titillating and suited to your unique vulnerabilities.

While the movies may be entertaining—after all, you are the main character in most of them—they are not nearly as invigorating as real life because they are predictable. Your gremlin wants you to watch the movies. He wants to keep you afraid of the unpredictability of real life. He prefers the illusion of predictability to the adventure of real life because he knows that excessive predictability leads to boredom, then the blahs, then the blues, then the dead zone, and eventually to a failure to thrive. Mired in your mind, you will eventually forget that there is any other reality. Your gremlin is hell-bent on dampening your pure Connection to your own Authentic experience of your own existence. He doesn't want anything to get to your Heart. He wants you trapped in your mind, watching movies of life.

Whence do he and his inspiration come? I don't know. But he's right there in your mind.

Play within your mind. Enjoy it. Watch a movie from time to time, but enter the world of mind with choice and clarity, remembering that you are not your thoughts, your feelings, your beliefs, your Hypnotic Pre-Convictions, your Habitual Behavior Patterns, or the roles you play. You are the one inside that body whose eyes are following these words. You are right here, right now, peering out through those eyes. Hello in there, from me in here. Nice to be here with you. The Natural You is the "experiencer," the Observer. At its core is your Heart, and your Heart is composed of true love. When you experience pleasure and peace, the essence of the experience is felt within your Heart. That essence is true love.

Your Heart is pure. What sort of experiences do you want to send its way—to Connect it to? You are the conduit.

If, in any breath's worth of time, your *Intention* is to truly *Connect* to your experience, and if you *Respect* the opportunity to do so, and if you take care with the *Environment* in which you wish to form the connection, then maybe, just maybe, you'll have an *Authentic*, unhampered Experience of your Heart and your very own existence.

Chapter 17

Authenticity

Al Carson was a near master of contentment—its creation, its preservation, and, when need be, its rapid restoration. When I was a little boy, he was huge and powerful in my eyes. A distant figure with flashing eyes and a dancing smile, he wore suit coats that were warm to the touch, and he smoked Max Seller cigars. Al Carson was my dad. We lived in the same house but in different worlds.

As I grew taller Al grew shorter and balder and more wrinkled, but his disposition stayed as light, vibrant, and clear as the sparkle in his eyes. His anger rarely surfaced, but when it did he was transformed—like Clark Kent into Superman, only quicker, because he didn't have to change clothes first. It happened suddenly, in the blink of an eye, and lasted only a few seconds—as if a switch had been tripped. His upper lip twitched, his teeth flashed bright white, and light shot out of his eyes. He grew taller and broader on the spot, he looked lethal and cocksure, and he moved like lightning. It was beautiful. It made me quake with fear and shiver with delight all at once, even when I was the object of the fire in his soul. It happened only once or twice a year, but it was worth the wait.

Al touched me in anger only twice. He slapped my face both times. I'm not big on hitting, and I feel that causing others pain is pretty much an across-the-board bad idea, but in both those instances I had it coming. In fact, I should have been drawn and quartered, but that wasn't Al's way. He figured my life was mine, and his was his, so he got miffed only if I interfered with him, and stayed angry only until the interference was cleared up. That sort of efficiency and Authenticity in intention and action are rare. They lend clarity and simplicity to life. For me, Al was a raw living example of staying current with one's emotions—anger, love, sadness, joy.

Again, lest I be misunderstood, I am NOT encouraging you to physically—or verbally, for that matter—express your anger willy-nilly, without care for other people's feelings and their property. I *am* encouraging swift, authentic expression, coupled with common sense. Authenticity has two components:

First, in any breath's worth of time,
having your very own unique experience
uncontaminated by your ideas
***about* your experience**

and
second, living and expressing,
in word and deed,
the truth of who you are

There's a difference between dancing because you're *trying* to have fun and dancing because you're *having fun*. A raucous, impromptu, milk-out-your-nose belly-laugh isn't in the same ballpark of experience with putting on a phony happy-face. Hugging people with whom you'd rather just shake hands and say howdy doesn't make you a genuinely warm, open person. Living the truth of who you are entails matching your voice and facial expression to your internal experience. It takes courage, and once in a while it's foolhardy, but all in all it's a good default position.

Clearly, there are limits. To spray your venom on your spouse because your office colleague behaved like a brainless baboon doesn't make good sense, but *habitually* legislating against your Authentic experience deprives others of really getting to know you. Sure, your act may win critics' acclaim, but what about the Natural You behind your act? Are you ever felt, touched, heard from? Intimacy requires Authenticity, and Authenticity requires that you jump out from behind your act and land on your feet in front of another breathing, living, human being and essentially say, "Here I am! Want to join me?" It's a matter of reporting in simple sentences and with responsible semantics precisely what you are experiencing, and doing so in a way in which your inner experience is congruent with your outward appearance—in short, by matching your voice and facial expression to what you are feeling on the inside.

**To live the truth of who you are,
you must show yourself,
not simply describe yourself.**

Your gremlin will have innumerable considerations about such bold displays of selfhood. He may have you convinced that experiencing anger is mean or unladylike, that displaying sadness is a sign of weakness or dependency, that uncensored joy is immature, that living your sexuality is naughty.

As you continue to stroll and occasionally stumble through life, simply notice the emotions you experience and your Habitual Behavior Patterns in response to them. (If you want more information on habits for responding to emotions, consider reviewing pages 46–56 in the revised edition of *Taming Your Gremlin.*)

If you catch yourself in the act of being less than Authentic, consider *playing with options* (pages 108–129 in the revised edition of *Taming Your Gremlin*). Change for a change. Fool around. Become aware of any fear you have of being really true to yourself. Your Heart prefers the real thing. Do you really want to miss out on you being you?

Remember the continuum we discussed earlier in our chapter on Connection and our "What, Dear One, are you afraid of?" question. *Simply notice* your gremlin's chatter and any HPC that's in the way of your Authentic experience and expression of yourself. Attend to your fear as it plays through your mind and body, and for goodness' sake don't tell yourself you must change. Just experience your emotions and your fears regarding their expression.

Notice your fears with a sense of detachment; consider their validity based on the current situation. Then, for kicks, once in a while, just change for a change.

Authenticity isn't always easy for some people.

THE POWER OF NO

Do you know the hardest word in the Western hemisphere to pronounce? It's spelled N-O. You can learn a great deal about yourself just by observing your ability to say the simple word "no." You wouldn't think it would be so hard. After all, when you were just a rookie at this game of life, you learned how to talk. You learned to say "Dada" and "Mama," and now you use words like "Kafkaesque" and "epiphany" and "plethora." So what's so hard about the word "no"? When you were two you said it all the time. You stamped your feet and said it, probably in public places.

"Yes" is easy. But "no"? For most adults, that's another matter. We hardly ever say no without explaining why we said it. Yet we say yes all the time with no explanation at all.

Want to have some fun practicing being Authentic? Play with this one. Say "no" to somebody, and then just hush, breathe, and listen. Don't explain anything. Just breathe and relax. Just let the "no" be there, remembering that no is neither better nor worse than yes. It's often, simply, an honest expression of what's true for you. Really. When you and I tell the truth, life is simpler, and sometimes the truth is expressed with no. You can, of course, soften the no by saying, "No, thank you," if you'd like. It's not a cop-out—just mannerly.

Either way; I double-dog dare you, sometime soon when you're in the mood, to experiment. Simply say "no" or "no, thank you," hush, breathe, and listen. If this behavior is new to you, it will prove to be a subtly powerful growth experience. And besides, it's a small and simple way of being Authentic, and when you're authentic, you give other people permission to be authentic with you, and authenticity works. It works in friendships, it works in romantic relationships, and it works in business relationships. *Simply notice*, describe, hush, breathe, listen. And here's another phenomenon that's rife with inordinate meaning for many people: the expression of anger.

ANGER

Anger is energy. That is all. It is neither innately good nor innately bad. Just as there are no dirty words, just dirty minds, there is no bad anger—just bad actions. Sure, anger reddens faces and can be expressed destructively. It can also be invigorating, and often it changes things for the better.

In working with interpersonal systems such as families, businesses, and nonprofit organizations, I've noticed that once people see that anger can be expressed as easily as love, they save time, have more fun, and work together better.

In entrepreneurial endeavors, stifled anger leads to stifled creativity. It also leads to grumbling, time wasted in unproductive cliques, scapegoating, increased sick leave, tardiness, and job turnover—in short, poor morale. And poor morale is very, very expensive.

If your habit has been to scare yourself into habitually stifling your anger, blow the lid off once in a while and see how it feels. You'll get some ideas about lid-blowing in the upcoming section titled "Resolving Conflict Constructively." Needless to say, if you opt for this alternative, use some common sense and good manners. Damaging living things and property is rarely a noble act. By the same token, if your style has been to explode, try to describe with responsible semantics and simple sentences exactly what you feel. When you do so, match your voice and facial expression to what you are feeling. If you stay current with expressing your emotions, especially your anger, it won't build up. To stay current with expressing emotions, consciously choose to respond to them as you experience them in the current moment. This doesn't always mean expressing yourself. It may mean playing with other options (revised edition of *Taming Your Gremlin*, Chapter 8, pages 108–132), such as simply taking the time to fully experience your emotions and to *simply notice* their accompanying thoughts. The key is to get to choice rather than simply calling into play a Habitual Behavior Pattern (HBP). In encounters with others, if you do choose to experiment with *Authentic* expression, remember your SNDHBL and "peel the onion" system:

Simply Notice
Describe
Hush
Breathe
Listen

Match your voice and facial expression to what you're feeling on the inside.

From my experience, hanging on to anger causes far more damage to people and their relationships than does its rapid, respectful release. Play. *Play with options*. Notice how you tend to handle little irritations. Then, from time to time, whenever you're a little irritated or even outraged, try a new style of managing the feelings, remembering that there is no universal rule about the right way to do it. This is your life. It's your choice. Breath to breath, moment to moment, it's your choice. Don't make a new rule or form an expectation of yourself, lest your gremlin have one more stick to beat you with. Just make a choice and *play with options*.

Because the Authentic experience and expression of anger is so loaded for so many, let's spend a few moments discussing one of life's prevalent challenges: interpersonal conflict. I think it will lend an air of practicality to the issue of Authenticity.

RESOLVING CONFLICT CONSTRUCTIVELY

Interpersonal conflict is as natural as nighttime. It's woven through the fabric of even the most loving relationships.

Two of the people I admired most in the world were my late Aunt Anna and Uncle Nathan. The love between them was evident to all who witnessed it. They enjoyed each other immensely. And no matter how many people were in the room, their loving connection was obvious. But evidently they had their tough times, too.

Once, just before my marriage to Leti, Uncle Nathan and I were taking a walk. In his lilting tenor voice he said, "You know, Rick, when your Aunt Anna and I were first married, we lived in a very small apartment. We had a bedroom with a bed in it, a very small kitchen with a kitchen table and two chairs, and a living room with a couch. One night, your Aunt Anna got so mad at me that she went out and slept on that couch. The next night, I got so mad at your Aunt Anna that I went out and slept on that couch. And the next night we got so mad at each other, we both went out and slept on that couch." Conflict happens in the best of relationships.

Let's say you find yourself in a thorny conflictive situation. You don't like the way you're feeling. You're considering broaching the issue with the other party involved, but you're nervous about it. What should you do? Well, for one thing, practice what you've already learned about the I CREATE system. Have a clear Intention to Connect with Respect for the opportunity. Attend to the Environment in which you are going to discuss the issue at hand. Be Authentic by using responsible semantics and by matching your voice and facial expression to your inner experience, and remember to *simply notice, describe, hush, breathe,* and *listen.*

By now you know that I'm not big on hard-and-fast rules, but here are some points to ponder when next you find yourself in a conflict with another human:

1. Conflict is made hardest when we feel that our act is attacked. Let people you value imply overtly or covertly that you are less wise, angelic, talented, or thrilling than you would like to think you are, and you'll sure as shootin' want to deny or correct their skewed perception. Your style may be to disqualify them in your mind, to bully them

with blows or bellows, to out-articulate them, to pout, or to work it out. If the latter is your desire, it's important to step out from behind your act and live the truth—at least for a while. To do so, you first have to be honest with yourself about your act. Just ask yourself, "How do I want this person to see me, and what difference does it make?" Consider telling the person your answer to this question.

Consider, too, asking the person how he or she perceives you. If this person's perception is different from yours, ask yourself and the other person what you have done to inspire such an opinion, and reflect on the answers you get. This is the easy part. It's the part where you get to learn about what you're putting out. It can help you make a clear decision to shore up or drop your act before leaping off into the next few steps—which are a little tougher and require more guts, but are important.

2. Ask yourself what your motivation is for even considering raising the issue with the other party. Take a good look at your Intention to see if it's worth your effort. A good test is to consider stating your intention aloud to the person with whom you are in conflict. If your intention is too low-down or embarrassing to go public with, then your motivation is probably too self-serving to lead to intimacy or to an experience of pleasure, so you probably would be best served to stuff it. If you decide to proceed, express yourself in a way that is consistent with your intention. If, for example, you want to work through a conflict toward a better relationship with someone, say that to the person and go no further until the two of you have established this as your mutual intention.

By the same token, if all you want is to dump some negative feelings or prove yourself right and the other person wrong, be honest with yourself about your agenda, and don't pretend otherwise. It's fine to express yourself for the sole intention of getting something off your chest. In fact, it's commendable at times. But be honest about it. If this is your intention, however, make certain that you proceed with respect for people and their belongings. Remember that you are as transparent as the rest of us and that simply venting your feelings under the pretense of working things out will likely result in your coming off as a phony—a mean phony.

If, having taken an honest look at your intention, you discover that it is to work through the conflict to the point of new clarity and a good feeling between you and the other person involved, here are some further tips to consider.

3. Go slow. Breathe. Relax.

4. If you are fearful of the possible consequences of openly expressing yourself, look your fear squarely in the eye and ask yourself what is the worst that can happen. Consider making a statement regarding your fear to the other party in the encounter. You might, for example, try out your version of one or any combination of these statements:

"There is something that I want to discuss with you, but I'm afraid that you will throw a fit."

"Hear all of what I am saying, and really consider it before you respond."

"You're important to me, and I want us to remain friends, *and* there are some things you're doing that are driving me nuts."

"I'm angry with you. What is also true is that I respect you and value our relationship."

"I'd like to speak candidly with you, and I'd like our conversation to remain between us."

"I want to really listen to you, and I want you to listen to me."

"This may be a tough conversation for us because my tendency may be to talk ugly, and in the past we've both tended to be sarcastic when angry. As we have this conversation, let's make an effort to treat each other with love and respect."

"I'm hesitant to talk with you about a certain sensitive issue, but I don't like feeling what I'm feeling and would like to clear the air. Are you open to a frank discussion?"

Chances are that you are no saint, either, when it comes to handling conflict, so you might want to ask the other person if there is any particular behavior of yours he or she wants you to attend to during the encounter.

5. Concentrate on accurately expressing yourself rather than on controlling the other person's behavior. Use Responsible Semantics, and remember to peel the onion, using SNDHBL:

Simply Notice
Describe
Hush
Breathe
Listen

Trade in your desire to be right for a spirit of adventure. Open up to the possibilities inherent in an unpredictable encounter.

6. Listen more than you talk. There are no two ways about it: resolving conflict takes time and gentle reflection on what the

other person says and on what you really want to say. Set a comfortable tempo for the conversation, and care enough to seek clarification of the other person's thoughts and feelings.

If you don't have the time for this sort of qualitative conversation, then you don't have a healthy slice of what it takes to be a first-rate spouse, parent, coworker, supervisor, supervisee, or friend. Make time. Working through conflict not only can restore harmony in relationships but can move the relationship to a higher level of functioning, a deeper level of authenticity, and an expanded level of potential productivity.

7. Get in touch with what you feel and think, and express it. Separate what you actually feel and think from what you tell yourself you *should* feel and think, from what you imagine, and from self-righteous justifications of your opinion. Express yourself accurately, taking ownership of your thoughts, preferences, and emotions. Describe your thoughts and emotions as belonging to you and you alone. Describe your experience just as you would a painting or a piece of music. For example:

"I'm aware of being miffed when I find myself waiting for you."

"I tighten up and have a hard time listening to you when you're yelling."

"I love watching you walk."

"I feel tense around you."

"Your voice soothes me."

"I'd appreciate it if you would start noticing how often you criticize me."

"I like you."

"I feel good when I'm with you."

"I regret calling you a pea brain."

135

8. If the conflict unfolding is fueled by an annoying behavior of the other party, be certain to describe vividly the behavior to that person. Be descriptive but not judgmental. "I hate it when you act like a jerk" will be less well received than "I am angry that you interrupted me."

9. Communicate authentically and congruently without blaming or being whiny and self-effacing. That is, allow your voice, your facial expression, and your body to accurately convey what you're feeling. Express yourself fully and completely, with regard to both your feelings and your thoughts, but do so in a manner that respects other living things, their space, and their property. Yell if you must, growl if you must, cry if you want. But don't call people names, hurl curses, pout, or bust up property.

10. Remember where you end and all else begins: that miraculous sheath known as your skin. If you feel defensive, say so. If you can't for the moment let go of a desire to win, say so, and suggest a specific time to talk again.

11. Be open to feedback even if it smarts. Almost anything that is said about you is in some way true. Conflict represents an incredible opportunity for personal growth.

12. If it is possible, suggest a solution, but remember that resolving a conflict doesn't always mean coming to an agreement. Sometimes an agreement simply isn't possible. In my almost four decades of work with families, couples, and organizations, I have been gratified to see how often open expression and wholehearted listening defuse conflict without any obvious agreement being reached.

13. If, after doing an honest character check with yourself, you notice that your true motivation is to be right, to win, or to

136

simply infuriate the other person, you might try being sassy. An eight-year-old Little Leaguer whose batting stance I was attempting to modify stopped me dead in my tracks with this line: "If you're so smart, why ain't you rich?"

Authenticity is essential to intimacy. But some folks fear both, primarily because they fear change. Like it or not, a human relationship is a system, and like any system, to be healthy it has to be dynamic, not static. Relationships are supposed to change, like individuals. In my work as a family therapist I have often heard the phrase "He (or she) is no longer the person I married." My initial thought is almost always "Of course not. Did you really expect him (or her) to stay exactly the same?"

Have you stayed the same? I haven't. A lean 165 pounds now, not so long ago I weighed 8 pounds, 7 ounces. And, though it's hard to fathom now, when I was eighteen I came within one shot of tequila of having indelibly carved in ink on my right forearm a tattoo of a red serpent wound around a silver saber. Above the design there was to be a waving red banner, proudly announcing the era's motto of macho mania: "Death Before Dishonor."

I'm glad I didn't get it done. It wouldn't have set well with my mother and father then, or my clients now. I didn't deserve it anyway. I wasn't a Marine. And while I'm not a big advocate of dishonor, for all I know, in a pinch I'd choose it over death, and pinch or not, I just might choose it over severe pain. This is true today. I guess it wasn't true then. It may not be true tomorrow. I change. I notice I change, sometimes out of conscious choice, but more often out of a sort of osmosis after some abrupt turnabout in my perception of myself, of humankind, or of the universal order of all and everything. People change, and so do relationships.

The monster of the mind—your gremlin—loathes the true dynamic nature of life. He'd rather have you relate to life out of fear of change. He'd rather have you watch the pictures *about* life stored in the warehouse of your mind than have you be *in* your life. Some people fake orgasms; other people fake relationships. Live exclusively in your mind, and you'll fake your whole life. Your gremlin will love it, but your Heart will miss out.

Where relationships are concerned, far more damage is done by resistance to change than by change itself. For any system, including a human relationship, to be healthy, it must be dynamic: open to new inputs. One of the healthiest vehicles for providing these inputs is Authenticity. Authentic communication is a primary means for keeping a relationship vibrant and healthy.

KNOWING AND KNOWING ABOUT

There is more to Authenticity than accurately and congruently expressing yourself. Living authentically means being willing to have your own unique experience rather than some trumped-up idea of what you think your experience should be. Remember, your mind doesn't *know*—it simply *knows about*. This speaks to the difference between information and true knowledge.

Bruce's primary relationship was with his mind. He piddled around in it for hours, pulling out file boxes, digging out old folders, and sometimes just wandering up and down the aisles until, sure enough, he encountered the monster. Then the torment would begin: remorse, self-loathing, trying to figure out why he had "made a mess of his relationships," and allowing his gremlin to convince him he would never change.

It never occurred to Bruce that his relationships to others were contaminated not by some despicable toxic character flaw but rather by the fact that he was emotionally unavailable, preferring to hang out in the warehouse of the mind.

Because Bruce feared life, he preferred to think *about* it

rather than risk being in it. The unpredictability of the real thing was much too threatening, though it had been a long time since he had given it much of a chance. His mind had been his closest friend for years.

Bruce and his mind had solidified their relationship nearly fifty years before, when things in his family of origin were filled with criticism and anger. In those days, lost in the world of mind, Bruce lived in fantasy—envisioning himself as a super-hero, a world-class athlete, a rock star. As time went on he developed other mind channels that he'd tune into.

The real world seemed so scary, and he, because of all the harsh criticism (from his parents and, before long, his gremlin) was so unsure of himself, that it was simply easier to live in his mind. It was dark and unpleasant in there at times, and there was that monster who lived there, but still it was more predictable than the real world. It was easier to handle—or so it seemed, though—and this is the sad part: until Bruce and I met he had never really thought about it. He'd lived in his mind so long that he didn't even know he was doing so or that he had a choice about how much time to spend there. At fifty-five, Bruce was a frightened little boy living life in the warehouse of his mind.

You can imagine the welcome relief Bruce felt as he simply began to gain control of his *spotlight of awareness* and as he woke up to the fact that he had a choice in each breath about what to pay attention to. Of course, we had more work to do, going back into the warehouse together to complete some unfinished business with the "dad" in Bruce's mind, and with Bruce's gremlin.

While spending more time connecting with the real world was unpredictable and therefore scary at first, it didn't take Bruce long to recognize that the line between fear and excite-ment is very thin. Once he began to feel the excitement, his motivation to really enjoy his life expanded exponentially, making our work together easier. Bruce now has an uncompromising Intention to Connect. To say he Respects the opportunity to fully experience his existence is putting it mildly. As for Environment—if it warms his Heart, terrific; if not, he'll leave or do his best to modify it. Regarding having his own genuine Authentic experience—he'll settle for nothing less. I am inspired by Bruce's commitment to being fully alive in each moment.

Having your own Authentic firsthand experience of your existence is essential to maximum experience and to maximum expression.

In the words of the phenomenal guitar artist Carlos Santana, "When you play from your heart, all of a sudden there is no gravity. You don't feel the weight of the world, of bills, of anything. That's why people love it. Your so-called insurmountable problems disappear, and instead of problems, you get possibilities."

Living I CREATE requires playing from the Heart, surrendering to the possibility that in any moment, a clear Intention to Connect with Respect in an Environment suited to Authenticity will result in a positive experience. I don't use the term "surrender" lightly, here.

Surrender requires a lot of Trust—trust in the process.

Chapter 18

Trust

Trusting I CREATE isn't easy at first. It requires lessening one's attachment to rigidly directing an outcome and replacing that attachment with trust in an infallible process.

The difficulty is that you won't discover its infallibility, nor yours in using it, until you give it your best effort. You'll be best served to do so without overthinking. Your mind will want to think it over—assess the what-ifs. Your gremlin will, of course, do everything in his power to frighten you away from practicing. Gaining the confidence to live I CREATE comes from practice.

I've had people say to me about experimenting with new behavior or taking on certain other challenges, "I'd try, but I just don't have the confidence." It's a screwy outlook. It implies that confidence is like good genetics or good luck—that it just sort of hits you or it doesn't. Not so. Confidence is more like a set of rippling abdominals. You have to put out effort in order to gain it.

To say "I can't do it because I don't have the confidence" is putting the cart before the horse. You build confidence by taking risks—calculated risks based on underpinnings of self-respect, realism, and a willingness to accept imperfect attempts as part of the process.

I'd like to suggest what I think will be an enjoyable way for you to practice I CREATE. It's a game I made up many years ago called Reminiscing. I offer it with the recognition that this sort of interactive experience is not everyone's cup of tea; handled poorly, it can feel rather contrived.

Back in 1975, when Leti and I had just purchased our first home, our next-door neighbors welcomed us by including us in a neighborhood dinner party. We were a little anxious, given that we were the newest to the neighborhood and younger than most of the other invitees, but we appreciated being included and were looking forward to meeting our new neighbors. After dinner, the hostess asked what she thought was a provocative question: "Given unlimited possibilities, what four famous people from history would we each most like to have dinner with?" We could pick anybody. I was first, and I proudly said, "Groucho, Harpo, Chico, and Zeppo." No one said much.

The woman to my right proudly announced, "Mozart, Gandhi, Picasso, and, of course, our Lord and Savior Jesus Christ." I fought my impulse hard. During the next second or two, I bit my cheek, gnawed my tongue, and held my breath. Then, no longer able to contain myself, I blurted out, "Do you mean the Jeffrey Hunter–looking Jesus with blond hair and blue eyes, or the real skinny Jewish-looking one?" A gentleman across the table started to laugh, but stifled it. Then there was a lot of throat clearing. That was in October. In December, when Leti and I were the only ones in our neighborhood to decorate our home with Happy Hanukkah and a neon "Judah Maccabee Rules," I felt sure they were saying, "That explains it."

Suggesting games and experiential activities is risky. It can be awkward for participants. But hey—the fact that you and I have hung together thus far suggests that we like each other enough to hold hands and take an unpredictable leap into the future. Besides, we're going to make what follows meaningful by maintaining a clear desire to learn, right? What is more, we will operate within the boundaries of a good intention and fair play.

REMINISCING

The game, again, is called Reminiscing, and it's a chance to practice I CREATE and to practice trusting the process. It's an opportunity to experiment with being at choice with entering the world of mind and to practice taming your gremlin on the spot. Here are the guidelines:

1. Bunch up. Get your body near one or more folks you enjoy. Relax and breathe. Open yourself up to the possibility of pleasure and enhanced potential, and then go to the next step.

2. Pick one or more of the items listed in item 8 about which to reminisce. Everyone present can share his or her experience on a common theme. If you prefer, select a few items on the list, write them down on slips of paper, drop them into a hat, and have each person draw one on which to reminisce aloud. If you choose this method, don't draw your topic until it's your turn to reminisce. Otherwise, you might be tempted to spend time mentally rehearsing instead of listening to others.

3. If you are the one doing the reminiscing, go slowly. Reflect and breathe. Begin by making a statement or three about what you're thinking or feeling at the moment, and then dive into reminiscing. Go by choice into the world of mind, specifically to your history channel. Give nary a thought to being profound. Talk for at least three minutes but no more than ten. Steer away from making points

about life on planet earth, and avoid generalizations. Don't pontificate. Simply report your experience as you recall it, i.e., SNDHBL.

4. *Simply notice, describe, hush,* and *breathe,* over and over. Allow yourself to remember your thoughts and feelings regarding the event(s) about which you are speaking. Use "I" a lot. Recall the details of your experience—what you saw, what you heard, what you felt, what you thought, and even what you were wearing, if you remember.

   Don't be obsessive about sticking with your topic. Just use it as a starting point. If, as you get into it, you find your attention drawn to a related memory, follow it, and let your mind and mouth ramble.

5. Throughout your oral reminiscing, pause from time to time, and share what your Here and Now experience is. What's it like to be you, telling your story? *Simply notice, describe, hush,* and *breathe.* If you're aware of your breathing becoming shallow, of feeling anxious, of censoring, or of your gremlin on the scene, share that as well. After you have completed your tale, take a moment to reflect on the impact the event you spoke about had on you. It needn't have blown you out of the water or changed your life. Simply reflect on the impact, whatever it was, and describe it to those present.

6. Now, take another moment to share what it was like to tell your tale to those present. For example, comment on what you felt when you began to tell your story, and how you felt as you got into it. If you heard your gremlin blowing and going, what did he (or she) say? If you found yourself wanting to impress or entertain, to whom were you giving the power to judge you?

7. As you listen to other folks reminisce, relax and enjoy the process. Allow yourself to be fully present by keeping your breathing clear and paying attention—the same sort of attention you would pay to a good movie or to a piece of music. To enjoy a movie you don't have to try hard. By the same token, if you're talking to the person next to you the whole time, you'll miss the movie. To enjoy a movie, you simply relax and gently cast your awareness on the movie. This same sort of gentle attentiveness is required for good listening. This gives you the chance to learn to use your ears with the same refined proficiency with which most of us have learned to use our mouths.

8. Here are a few topics with which to experiment. You can also have a big time making up your own.

   One of the first times you heard a particularly impactful word or phrase

   Your first romantic kiss

   A pair of shoes you owned as an adolescent

   Your life, as traced through automobiles with which you've had a relationship

   A flirtation you've had

   Your first job

   A time as a preadolescent when you were proud of yourself

   The first time you fell head over heels in love

   A special experience with one of the people present

   An early friendship

   An enemy from your past

   A personal injury or illness you've experienced

   Your circumstances five years ago

   A special time with your dad or mom

A fight or bitter conflict in your past

Something you wish you'd done differently

A time you took a risk

A personal accomplishment within the past year

A sad time in your life

Your teenage idol (or idols) and why you think you
selected them

A joyful time in your life

Your favorite clothes from the past

A family gathering

An encounter with a celebrity

Your first day of school

Acts you've used in your life and how you've selected
them

Far be it from me to ask you to do something I wouldn't do,
so I'll share a reminiscence.

My theme of thought right now and in most of my waking
moments lately evolves from my desire to please you, my agent,
and my publisher. Toward this end I've been reading about
writing. I read that "a good writer explodes onto the paper."
I'm exploding onto the paper. Whammo! Blammo! Splat!

I admire phrases that imply action, like "he fell bleeding
onto the ground" or "his hand found the V of her crotch and
pressed against it" or "climb it and twirl" or the granddaddy of
them all: "they fucked."

"Fuck" was a shoo-in for commanding attention until about
twenty years ago, when it was yanked from its hideaway in the
dark alleys of men's minds and tossed willy-nilly onto the main
street of everyday banal banter. Overexposure hasn't been good
for "fuck." Before "fuck" went public, it held a special place in
my mind and heart. It was a no-nonsense word. It was sinister

146

and mysterious and powerful. It implied adventure. Most everybody knew about it, some acted on it, but only the bawdy
and irreverent said it aloud. The first time I heard "fuck" I was
seven, and my nine-year-old hero, Norman, mumbled to his
snot-nosed tag-along little sister, Barbara, the words "Go fuck
a duck." It made no sense. What was a "fuck"? I felt the impact
all the way down to my bones. I'm sure my eyes grew wide and
my mouth gaped open. I knew "fuck" was big, bad stuff, but I
didn't know what. I asked Norman. He said, "It's when you
poke somebody with your peter." I knew about peters (tally-
wacker, wanger, twig-and-berries), but I had heard nothing of
poking people with them.

In the next few days, I told almost every kid on the block to
"go fuck a duck." In the midst of a snowball fight with SueAnn
and Melissa, the two girls who lived across the street, I bellowed it out at the top of my lungs. Frank, my brother (nearly
ten years my senior), heard me, came out, and hauled me into
the house. He sat me down and told me not to tell people to
"go fuck a duck." I could tell he meant business. This inten-
sified the mystery in my mind. That a phrase could warrant
a surefire command from my otherwise mild-mannered big
brother baffled and thrilled me all at once. Frank asked me if I
knew what "fuck" meant. I said yes. He didn't ask for details or
offer new information. I'm glad. If my mental picture of "fuck"
had become any more vivid than "poking someone with your
peter," my circuits would have blown, sure enough. Frank released me on probation, and I went back outside.

The sinister quality of "fuck" has simmered down in my
mind since that day fifty-something years ago. But the intrigue
and intrinsic power of the word have remained. I respect "fuck"
and don't like it tossed around lightly. It's a first-class exple-
tive. It's top-notch and shouldn't be wasted on some small-
potatoes dilemma, minor upset, or second-class enemy. "Fuck"
is to be savored and, when needed, issued forth with regard for
its character.

When you play Reminiscing, it's important to simply notice your own process, including your fears and vulnerabilities, and to consider sharing them. I'm noticing, for instance, my hesitancy in having the word "fuck" appear here. I sincerely want this book to help you, not offend you.

I've just sought counsel. I called a good friend of mine for advice. She's a dignified lady of seventy-seven. She's honest, she's always willing to speak her mind, she never says words like "fuck," and she changes television channels when others do. I shared with her what you've just read. She said, "It's a true story. It makes a point. I hope you use it."

Now you try it. As you dive into this activity, live I CREATE.

REMINDERS

- Get your Intention clear. The choice of where to focus your awareness is yours. In every moment you are a devotee: you devote your attention to something. Among your choices are your breathing, the people and things that surround you, the world of mind (you'll want to go there to tap into a memory about which to reminisce), your gremlin's chatter. Where you place your awareness is up to you. The key is *choice*—and clear *Intention*.

- As speaker and listener, consciously choose what you wish to *Connect* with in each moment. Gently guide your awareness back and forth from the world of mind, to your body, to your immediate surroundings. As the speaker, from time to time, comment on each.

- Dive into the experience. *Respect* the opportunity inherent in each breath's worth of time. Breathe, and keep your internal metronome set at a comfortable pace.

- Attend to the *Environment* in which you're playing the game. Remember that your Environment is everything from your Heart out, including your state of mind.

- Be *Authentic*. Match your voice and facial expression to your inner experience. If you are the speaker, describe your experience accurately. Let your inner experience be what it will be. Don't *try* to make it other than it really is.

- *Trust* the process. Surrender. Breathe. Go slowly. Trust

that if your Intention is to Connect fully, and you do so with Respect for those present and for your reminiscence, and if you take care with seeing that your Environment supports your Intention to Connect with Respect, you will have an unabashed, all-out, richly rewarding, *Authentic Experience* of you and your life.

Chapter 19

Experience

The quality of your breath-to-breath experience and the quality of your life are inextricably linked. Your Heart is both a recipient of experiences you provide it and your guide.

Your Heart is the essence of who you really are: It longs to be felt. In moments when you feel your Heart, your experience is greatly enriched. When you are in touch with your Heart, you feel satisfied, fulfilled, loving, and loved, even in times of loss and upheaval. Your Heart lies behind your breath, and as with your breath, even if we dissected you, we could not see it. Yet it is there.

Your Heart has been with you since you arrived on the planet. It is your best friend, and when you feel lonely, empty, deeply despondent, or disconnected, it is a connection to your Heart you long for. You've felt your Heart often, if only subtly.

When next you experience simple pleasure, whether you are walking in the woods, watching your kids play, stroking your lover's hair, or basking in the afterglow of just having accomplished something you're proud of, take two breaths' worth of time to notice not just the circumstances engendering the pleasure but the essence of the feeling itself. It's in the center of your chest, behind your physical heart, and beneath your breath. It's your Heart.

The experience may be slight at first, but as you begin to attend to it, it will expand in your awareness ever so slightly. It's like gently breathing on a flame. As you notice your Heart and as you begin to notice what resonates with it and what doesn't, you can let your Heart begin to guide you. Constrict or crimp your breathing, and you limit your ability to feel your Heart.

Your Heart is like a radar beam. It will guide you toward experiences it finds satisfying and away from those it doesn't. It can tell you where to spend time, whom to hang out with, even what to eat. Your Heart is pure. What sort of experiences do you want to provide your Heart? Remember, you are the conduit.

I CREATE is a road map for making certain you are doing your part to maintain your connection between your Heart and your breath-to-breath experience.

In the name of protecting you from pain, your gremlin, who dwells in the world of mind, will do his best to scare you into clinging to the illusion of predictability and to pictures of what happiness is. He will use what's stored in the mind to berate and frighten you. He'll lead you to make great meaning where there is none. Even though satisfaction is a natural state already within you, your gremlin will work full time to convince you to strive for it via material goods, certain traits, particular attitudes, even a particular personality style.

But you can't experience happiness and try to produce it at

the same time. To try to produce something you have to have an idea about it, and the idea will interfere with your pure experience. Happiness is no more than the experience of true love, and true love already exists within you. It doesn't need to be produced.

So, if our Heart is so wonderful, why do we spend so much time avoiding it by stumbling around in the mind? It's because we've become so lost in the mind that we've lost touch with what's real. I CREATE is a system for reawakening to the reality of your own experience of yourself and of the world, and for beginning to open yourself to the satisfaction and peace already within your Heart. Your Heart wants to be felt, and within you is an innate drive to feel it.

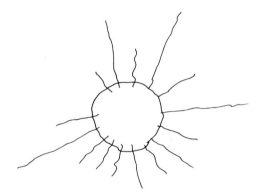

Chapter 20

A Breathing Meditation: An Opportunity to Practice I CREATE

I teach most of my clients and workshop participants a breathing meditation. Meditation is a process for selectively, with effort (not strain), focusing one's spotlight of awareness on something while relegating all else to the background of one's experience. Some people meditate using mantras, others on images, still others on gathas (short poems). Some people use candles; others use counting.

Since my most important relationship—and yours, too—is with the breath, I prefer a breathing meditation.

Your body is finite and will decay. Within it, thus far, anyway, is an infinite force that keeps your body functioning. That infinite force and your finite body have come together to form the entity that answers to your name. They are connected by your breath. Your breath is worth attending to. In preparing to do some lectures in Israel recently, I discovered a lovely bit of information. In Hebrew, the word for soul is *nashama,* and the word for breath is *nashima.* Isn't that delightful?

When I teach my clients to meditate on their breathing, I personally guide them; therefore, they usually surrender to what comes their way, and they enjoy the experience. I then suggest that they practice meditating each morning on their own until we get together again. It is not uncommon, however, when I next meet with them, for me to hear comments such as these:

"I couldn't quiet my mind."

"I kept getting distracted."

"I was so impatient."

"I got sleepy."

"My gremlin went wild."

The problem? Expectations. Concepts. Pre-Convictions, Hypnotic and otherwise. Instead of simply having and accepting their own Authentic experience, they are listening to their mind's trumped-up ideas *about* what meditation *should* be like. Whether you have a blissful time in meditation or a grueling "I'd rather be anywhere but here" experience is not the point. The point is to do it: to practice gently directing—and, when necessary, redirecting—your *spotlight of awareness* to your breathing. That is, to employ relaxed concentration to establish and reestablish your breathing as the foreground of your experience and to relegate all else to the background of your experience.

In a few moments I will offer you a breathing meditation. If you choose to practice it, it will serve you in several ways. It is an opportunity for you to surrender and accept your very own Authentic experience. It will show you what a pest your gremlin is. It will give you a brief and simple overview of how I CREATE works and, more important, how to work

155

I CREATE. And it will serve as a system for establishing the current moment as your home base. It will also help you gain control of your spotlight of awareness.

There will be distractions: sounds outside the room, your thoughts, and physical sensations. All of this is fine. Distractions are to be expected and are an important part of the process. That is why the process is called practice. That is exactly what you will be doing—practicing. You will close your eyes, locking yourself in with your mind and with your gremlin, and you will practice focusing your spotlight of awareness on your breathing while your gremlin keeps on chattering. Doing so will require effort. It does not require strain. It definitely requires practice. Think of your morning practice of meditation as just that—practice.

You close your eyes, and you lock yourself in with your mind, your gremlin, and your breathing, and you begin to practice. You practice exercising gentle control over your awareness and keeping your breathing in the foreground of your experience while relegating your mind, your gremlin's haranguing, and all else to the background of your experience. You enter these practice sessions with no expectations, and certainly no illusion that your mind will stay in the background of your experience for more than a few breaths.

I CREATE has been described as a method for living life as a meditation. It is a system for realizing, in the purest sense of the word, the sacredness of every moment. To lead life as a meditation, it is helpful to establish the present moment as your home base and to gain gentle control over your *spotlight of awareness* early in your day. From my experience, formal meditation—often called sitting or practicing—is the most efficient and satisfying way to accomplish this.

Practicing in the morning before you leap off into your day is a marvelous way to set the tone for a gratifying all-day experience. How long you formally practice each morning may vary, but I suggest a minimum of fifteen minutes, and much longer if possible. But even a very few conscious, fully enjoyed breaths is a precious gift to give yourself. You'll want a comfortable cushion or chair to sit on. If you do use a chair, place your feet flat on the floor and keep your spine at least fairly erect, but not uncomfortably so. Be certain not to scrunch up your torso, since you will want to make liberal and lively use of your abdomen as you inhale and exhale fully throughout your practice. If you are an experienced meditator, a relatively accomplished yogi or yogini, or just really limber, you may wish to grant yourself a traditional posture, such as the lotus. For our purpose here and now, however, that is not at all necessary.

In some meditation traditions, practitioners keep their arms slightly away from the sides of their bodies, palms up, and they form a circle using the thumb and forefinger of each hand. You may experiment with this if you wish. If you prefer, simply place your hands in your lap, palms up. During your practice, your Intention will be to Connect with your breathing.

Each new breath that comes your way is a gift. Savor each one by *simply noticing* it and appreciating it, and then exhale it fully. With no real effort on your part, another will enter your body. Enjoy it as well. They come one at a time. Notice, you can't take the next one until you have taken in and released the current one.

Begin by dropping your eyelids and then exhaling fully and completely, blowing out the last bit of air in your lungs. As air comes rushing back into your lungs, place your spotlight on the air and its path in and out of your system. Continue to gently follow the path of your breath in and out, simply breathing at a pace that is comfortable for you, and making certain to take in all the air you want and to exhale fully. As you exhale pull your abdomen in, and as you inhale allow your abdomen to push outward.

When your awareness drifts into your mind, to your gremlin, or to other distractions, simply gently direct it back to your breathing. That is all, and that is plenty. All you are doing is *practicing* gently controlling your spotlight of awareness and in the process establishing the Here and Now as your home base for the day. Remember, meditation is all practice.

Your gremlin may come charging in wearing combat boots, shouting obscenities, and berating you for wasting time, being a nobody, and even telling you you're a lousy meditator. If that doesn't work, he might simply opt for the old flapping of arms and screeching "the sky is falling!" number. Your awareness will drift. Your gremlin will make every effort to seduce you into the world of mind. At some point, in all likelihood, you will notice yourself lost in worry, analysis, considerations about the day before you, and the random ramblings of the mind:

"Whatever happened to Snooky Lanson and the rest of the *Your Hit Parade* gang?"

"What was really behind my decision to give up bowling?"

Your attention may be drawn to an itch or to other physical sensations. This is natural, and neither good nor bad. At the point at which you notice your spotlight of awareness has drifted from your breathing, simply redirect it there, and again begin to follow the path of your breath in and out of your body.

In all likelihood, eventually you will settle down. Let your thoughts be like clouds. As you notice them, simply let them drift by, and drop your awareness back to your breathing. Allow the seat or cushion you are sitting on to support you. Keep your posture comfortably erect. Each time you notice your awareness has drifted, simply remember that your *Intention* is to *Connect* with your breathing. At that point, simply direct your awareness back to your breathing.

In order to fully connect, you must *Respect* that what you are spending time connecting with is worth the time you are spending connecting with it. After all, these are precious moments of your life you're spending. Once they are gone, they're gone. There's a whole world out there. Is meditating on your breathing really how you want to spend some of your time?

For me, absolutely. Meditating on my breathing often leads me to a beautiful experience beyond my breath and deeper than my breath. I love this experience, so I enter meditation with a great deal of respect for the opportunity. I respect each breath as a gift that, as near as I can tell, I've done nothing to deserve. And I like the effect meditating on my breathing in the mornings has on my inner experience throughout the day. In other words, I respect my breathing and the experience produced by meditating on it. I like the way meditating on my breath makes me feel.

If your *Intention* is clearly to *Connect* with your breathing, and if you *Respect* your choice to connect with it, it simply makes sense to attend to the *Environment* in which you are making and enjoying the connection. In front of a blaring television set? Probably not. In the middle of a busy day? Maybe. The truth is, I'll take meditation wherever I can get it, but ideally in a relatively quiet place where I can sit comfortably— with a clear *Intention*, a solid *Connection*, *Respect* for the process and the benefits, in an *Environment* suited to the activity at hand.

And let's you and I not be hung up on some idea of meditation, or of what a *good* practice session is. We don't want anybody's ideas, including our own, interfering with our pure *Authentic* experience. We want the real stuff—the real McCoy—not our ideas about it. Surrender to the process. *Trust* I CREATE and yourself, and enjoy a satisfying *Experience*.

Just as your outer world is best experienced and examined directly, so is your inner world. It doesn't require tags and labels. Once the richness of a breath's worth of time has passed, it may go into the warehouse of your mind as a memory and be filed away. But every moment we spend in the file room seeking it is a moment away from the richness of pure experience.

Your gremlin will attempt to use what's lying around in your mind—layers of concepts, assumptions, and expectations—to distract you from the purity of your existence. But you're on to him. *Simply notice* him, then redirect your awareness to your breathing.

Before coming out of your meditation and lifting your eyelids to charge off into your daily life, take a few moments to notice the surface of your skin. Notice the air on your skin, and your clothes on your skin. Your skin is a miraculous organ. It is a sensitive receptor and a boundary. Remember,

Every experience you have in this life occurs

within the boundary defined by your skin.

Events occur around you, and you participate

in many of them.

But your experience of those events occurs

within the boundary defined by your skin.

Within the boundary defined by your skin, you are drawing in these words through your eyes. Within the boundary defined by your skin, you get wrought up, bummed out, turned on, turned off, wired, and wrung out. From within the boundary defined by your skin, you decide what to pay attention to—what to meditate on, moment to moment, and breath to breath. The benefits of meditation are tremendous in terms of peace, clarity, and establishing the current moment as your home base. But the most wonderful benefit, the most practical gift of meditation, is that you, having established the present moment as your home base through formal practice, and having gained gentle control over your awareness, can reap the benefits of clarity all day long. And when you get distracted and knocked off center, which will happen many times during the day, you are never more than one breath away from returning to your home base in the Here and Now.

Think of the present moment—that is, what is going on in your body and what you can experience in your immediate surroundings with your sensory receptors— as your home. Within your home, you have a very peaceful, quiet room. That room is your breathing.

Being solidly grounded in your home base, maintaining access to your special room within, and gently controlling your awareness as you move through life make life a meditation. As I stroll (and stumble) through life I want to be grounded in something real, like my breath. No matter where I go, it's right there with me. I like the experience of staying in touch with my breathing and having a clear sense of where I end and all else begins—that miraculous sheath known as my skin. I call this state of being Being Centered, and I recommend it to you.

Think of the world as a multidimensional movie you have been plopped down in the middle of. Remember that the most important relationship you have is with yourself, specifically with your own breath and your own Heart.

Chapter 21

I CREATE
as a Checklist

Being a professional inner guide is a strange way to make a living. Not much equipment is required, no stethoscopes or monkey wrenches. I am my primary tool.

My clients pay me to bring all of myself—my sensing abilities, my thoughts, my life experience, my emotions, and my skills—to bear on their behalf. I CREATE began as a checklist of guideposts by which I could assess the quality of my involvement with my clients. It worked so well that I almost immediately began applying it to virtually all my interpersonal relationships and soon to every activity in my life, from meditation to creative endeavors like writing this book. I've taught it to others as well.

I CREATE works. It's working in my life, and it's working in the lives of many people who have been interested enough to give it a go. Use I CREATE as a checklist by which you can, at any given moment, in the context of any given relationship with a human being, a project, a challenge, or an idea, assess to what extent you are doing your part to ensure that that relationship is truly fulfilling for you and any others involved. I CREATE is a formula for creating harmony, productivity, wellness, positive change, and a sense of well-being.

And I CREATE can help you tap into and channel the potential of others, such as employees and students and your children. I CREATE contains within it the keys to becoming a terrific lover. It can help you resolve conflict constructively, and relate without difficulty to difficult people. You can use I CREATE to alleviate anxiety, to bust out of the blahs and sling off the blues, to relieve your stress, to accumulate wealth, and to successfully and artfully express yourself.

- ✔ INTENTION
- ✔ CONNECTION
- ✔ RESPECT
- ✔ ENVIRONMENT
- ✔ AUTHENTICITY
- ✔ TRUST
- ✔ EXPERIENCE

Chapter 22

A Blast from the Past: Revisit and Re-Decide

It's amazing how many of our Hypnotic Pre-Convictions were firmly embedded in our minds in early childhood. Many of yours were drawn from what you witnessed and from how you were responded to by your parents and others in your family of origin. (On pages 123–129 in the revised edition of *Taming Your Gremlin*, there's an elaborate exercise for getting to choice with some of these notions.) Still other HPCs came to you from your experiences outside of your family of origin, even from your experiences with your early playmates.

On occasion, working through an HPC in depth is aided by what, in *Taming Your Gremlin*, I call Revisiting and Re-Deciding. Revisiting and Re-Deciding takes a little time, and while it relies on stepping back in time, and therefore into the world of mind, it is definitely an experiential process more than an intellectual one. It draws into play both insight and awareness but relies most heavily on the latter. A skilled facilitator helps. I often use Revisiting and Re-deciding in my office with clients, and the following case vignette will help you see how it works. I offer it because it is an elaborate illustration of some of the key elements you and I have been discussing. What follows will be especially helpful to inner guides such as psychotherapists and life coaches.

Russell and I first met a couple of years ago when I helped him and his wife work through some rough spots. When he came into my office last month, he was fretful and anxious. Quite definitely, he was dwelling at the uptight end of the imaginary continuum we discussed in Chapter 14. Russell's anxiety was evident. His breathing was quite shallow, he was pale, and he had prominent bags under his eyes from lack of sleep. Early in our session, Russell, a forty-year-old successful mortgage broker, mentioned that he was being considered for a promotion. When he added that two of his professional peers, a man and a woman, both slightly older than he but with less experience, were also being considered, his shoulders slumped. He looked down, and his breathing became even shallower. It was as if he were making himself smaller.

I asked Russell to notice his experience and describe it to me. He softly said, "I just know I won't be chosen." I asked Russell to keep his posture scrunched up the way it was and to make the same statement again. He again said, "I just know I won't be chosen." I asked him what he was feeling. He said he felt scared. I asked him to scare himself more and to do it aloud so I could hear him. He said again, "I'm just afraid I won't be chosen." He had the look of a scared kid, so I asked Russell how old he felt. He said, "Honestly? About five or six, I guess." I suggested that Russell close his eyes, shift his awareness into his imagination, and bring into his imagination an image of himself at five or six. He did.

I then asked Russell to take a good look at the child in his imagination—to notice precisely what the child was wearing and to pay especially close attention to the child's eyes and to the area surrounding his eyes. I asked, too, that Russell notice his own experience in the present moment as he looked at the child in his imagination. I suggested that he notice the setting in which he saw his younger self. In a few moments, tears began to roll down Russell's cheeks. His breathing became very shallow. I suggested that he relax his breathing and allow himself to feel what he was feeling. His lower lip began to quiver, and he continued to fight against his tears. I simply encouraged him to take in all the air he wanted, to exhale fully, and to entitle himself to his experience. I asked him to keep his eyes closed, and then I guided Russell through a dialogue with the youngster in his head.

When I guide this sort of Revisit and Re-Decide experience, I typically ask that my clients not speak aloud, emphasizing that this experience is for them, not for me. As they are having the imaginary dialogue, I occasionally intersperse instructions. I attempt to do so somewhat akin to how a good waiter operates. I want to guide my clients' experience without interrupting it, so my comments are whispered softly and only occasionally, usually when I notice a shift in their breathing or some other physical adjustment. These shifts clue me that they may be removing themselves from the experience, that their foreground is shifting, and I want to direct their *spotlight of awareness* back to the fantasy dialogue and occasionally to their own physical experience in the present moment.

My timed and whispered instructions to Russell were statements such as these:

"Be completely honest with the younger you."

☆

"Go beyond the point of predictability."

☆

"Allow yourself to be completely uncensored."

☆

"Breathe."

"Let my voice and other thoughts be background."

☆

"Allow the child to be the foreground of your experience."

☆

"Imagine a response from the child to you as an adult that

is just as forthright and heartfelt as yours to him."

☆

"Now, imagine yourself as the child."

☆

"Get a sense of the child's experience in the moment

you're seeing him."

Later, when I brought Russell out of the world of mind into the present moment, I asked him to report his experience to me. He explained that he had seen himself as a small boy standing with seven or eight other boys and a girl. Two other slightly older boys were picking teams for a sandlot baseball game. As was often the case, young Russell was the last chosen. In fact, he hadn't been chosen at all. He'd been left standing. He described in detail how alone, inadequate, and unwanted he felt. As it turned out, when Russell was a small child in Louisiana, he hung out with a whole tribe of neighborhood kids. He was the youngest, the smallest, and almost always the last chosen when teams were picked for the sport of the season. Through elementary and junior high school he had a slight build and short stature compared with his peers. Though his body shot up and filled out in his junior year of high school, his HPC of himself as physically inadequate and as the "one not chosen" was firmly embedded in his mind by then, and his gremlin kept it in play.

HPCs work in the same way racism and anti-Semitism do. Holders of these destructive ideas use exceptions to reinforce what they hold to be the truth. Once the HPC is in place, it reinforces itself by influencing outcomes. An old adage holds true here: Some people think they can, and some people think they can't, and they're both right. It's the old yin and yang thing—you know: the cheese shredder is also a sponge destroyer. HPCs don't always dictate experience, but they certainly influence it.

As Russell became aware of precisely how his gremlin was using his past to contaminate the present, his anxiety began to diminish. He still wanted the promotion badly and would no doubt be disappointed if he were passed over, but his present reality was no longer infused with the anguish and dread of the unchosen six-year-old. Before Russell and I parted ways for the day, I asked him to become very aware of his breathing, the surface of his skin, his musculature, his adult body in the present moment. I helped him re-center himself by taking him out of the world of mind and having him shift his spotlight of awareness back and forth between his breathing and his visual field.

Once Russell was firmly centered and grounded in the present moment, I suggested that he quite slowly make himself small once again, scrunching up his posture and lowering his eyes. He reluctantly agreed, and I had him in slow motion go back and forth between his scrunched up posture and his "centered in the present moment" posture. I asked that he imagine a continuum bounded by an image of himself in each posture and suggested that throughout the day he stay aware of where on the continuum, moment to moment, situation to situation, he was placing himself. He agreed.

I asked for more. I asked Russell to quite slowly, once again, make his body small, lower his eyes, and scare the hell out of himself, just as he had been doing at the beginning of our session. He said he didn't want to, leaned back, took a deep breath, and looked me in the eye.

I offer this session summary to you as a rather elaborate illustration of some of the key principles of the Gremlin-Taming

Method. My hope is that you will see clearly within it such elements as these:

- Simply noticing
- Choosing and playing with options
- Breathing and fully experiencing
- Accentuating the obvious
- Revisiting and re-deciding
- Making being centered a top priority and knowing that doing so is primarily an inside job
- The importance of remembering where you end and all else begins: that miraculous sheath known as your skin
- Breathing, as both a barometer and a regulator of inner experience
- Relaxing your attachment to your act
- Establishing the Here and Now as a home base from which you consciously direct your spotlight of awareness
- The Zen Theory of Change
- How HPCs contaminate the present with the past
- Realms of awareness
- Being in process

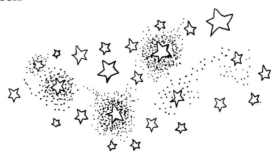

Chapter 23

The Power of Until Now

People often tell me about themselves using definitive phrases:

"I am a procrastinator."
"I'm always late."
"I'm terrible at remembering names."
"I'm a lousy artist."
"I can't manage money."
Etc.

Talk about psychic tattoos—HPCs of the first order. If you outwardly verbalize these or similar beliefs about yourself, I guarantee you they have played through your head day in and day out for years, and still are. Thank your gremlin.

Imagine the effect these Hypnotic Pre-Convictions have had on you. If your gremlin has you convinced you are a static human being, incapable of change, you won't change. But you're not static, and while accepting the psychic tattoos may give you an excuse for being late, forgetting names, or screwing up your bank account, the truth is that you can change if you want to.

If you've decided you can't remember names, may I suggest you're right. And you'll never be able to so long as that tattoo of the mind is in place.

When you next simply notice a self-limiting HPC being whispered into your ear by that low-down, ne'er-do-well gremlin of yours, consider playing with this option: Say to yourself simply,

"Until now I've done a lousy job with my finances."

or

"My tendency has been to be late."

or

"Until now my habit has been to . . . "

While replacing the self-limiting HPC with some positive affirmation such as "I'm a terrific money manager" might help, it's not the key to sending your gremlin scurrying. You want to change from the inside out, not merely develop a new and better HPC. The power to make a deep-seated change lies in your ability to *simply notice* the HPC—that is, to shine a bright *spotlight of awareness* on it in the very breath's worth of time in which it plays through your being. Simply notice the psychic tattoo for what it is—a hypnotic bit of hullabaloo that may well have been in place by the time you were six, and reinforced thousands of times since by your gremlin.

Once an HPC is stored in your warehouse of the mind, your gremlin can use it however and whenever he pleases to limit your creativity, your productivity—in short, you being you. The HPC influences your experience, and before long, your experience begins to support the HPC.

See your psychic tattoos for what they are. Every time you hear yourself make a statement to someone or to yourself about who you are or how you are, simply think the word "Whoa!" Then rephrase the Hypnotic Pre-Conviction in the manner I've suggested: "Until now. . . . ." The Natural You and your Heart will take care of the rest.

Chapter 24

Serving Your Heart

Self-awareness is a gift, and self-reflection can boost your personal potential, but self-absorption will lead to a feeling of disgruntled emptiness. It's important to take hold of that *spotlight of awareness* you control and to lovingly shine it out on others as often as you can. Notice others, their wants and their needs, and offer yourself to them. The true love within you is a gift you can share through action. To do so will fill you with gratification, and it can benefit humankind. Help out.

Regardless of how you choose to help, as long as your Intention is clear, you are in touch with your Heart, and you are doing what you choose to do in a manner consistent with your experience of true love, you will feel good and others will benefit. You can miss out on the fulfillment inherent in doing service for others by getting caught up in concepts *about* what loving behavior looks like. Don't. Instead, simply breathe, tap into the true love within your Heart, and let it manifest in your actions toward others.

If you are faithful to the natural experience of true love within you, you will feel terrific, and other people will benefit from the experience.

Serving your Heart will satisfy you. You can serve your Heart in two ways. First, you can serve it in the same way a devotee serves a master—by listening and responding to it and following its lead. You serve your Heart by taking the actions it leads you to take.

Second, you can serve your Heart by offering to others the true love that is its essence—by "serving it up," the way you would a big slice of cherry pie. Serving your Heart will satisfy you.

Service and servitude are not the same. Sacrifice is not what makes for good deeds; loving action is. Good works are pervaded by common sense and Intention, not by suffering. From my experience as a therapist and consultant, I want to emphatically announce that no single factor causes more damage and confusion in relationships than people taking excessive responsibility for one another's woes. Sometimes too much help is not helpful. A Vietnamese proverb speaks profoundly of the balance between taking care of yourself and doing service for others:

"While it is noble to help an elephant which has been stricken, it is foolish to attempt to catch one which is falling."

I'm grateful that my profession affords me daily opportunities to do service for others. Often I'm able to do so by using and teaching much of what I've shared with you.

Ruth came into my waiting room for her first visit. She was wearing a proper church-lady dress. Her hair was in a bun, and her face was all scrunched up as if she had gotten a whiff of something awful. She prissed into my interview room. Her steps were tiny and quick, and her back was rigor-mortis stiff.

174

She took a seat, placing her tiny little bottom so lightly on the couch that she barely dented it. I took a seat facing her.

Ruth sat with her thighs squeezed together, her elbows close to her sides, and her hands atop her patent leather purse. Pressing her thin lips together, she gave me a squinty-eyed tea party smile. We chitchatted for a moment, then I asked her what was up. She hemmed and hawed for a few seconds and then told me that her husband ignored her.

I asked her if she had ever made mud pies.

She asked me, "Will this help?"

I asked her, "Would what help?"

She said, "To talk about whether or not I've ever made mud pies."

I said that I didn't know but I thought it might.

She looked away.

I suggested she relax her breathing and allow herself to ramble.

She said, "I just don't know," and looked down at the floor.

I leaned forward, put my head even lower than hers, and looked up at her.

She looked away and said, "I just don't know if this will do any good."

I said, "What does 'any good' mean? What would be 'good'?"

She didn't answer.

I asked again, "What would be 'good'?"

She said, "Just to be happy, I guess."

I asked her if she was unhappy.

She said, "I suppose I am."

I said, "Say 'I am unhappy.'"

She said, "I am unhappy."

I said, "Say it again, and look me in the eye so that I get the message."

She looked at me and said, "I am unhappy. I am so very unhappy."

I said, "Relax your breathing and say it again."

She did. Tears came. She sobbed heavily for a long time. I took the purse from Ruth's hands and placed it beside her. She moved her hands to her face, and she cried and sputtered and breathed, and cried and sputtered and breathed some more. I handed her some tissues and moved onto the couch next to her, placing my hand on her back as she heaved with sadness. After a while she mumbled through her tears, "There has to be more."

I said, "Say 'I want more.'"

She did.

I said, "Say it louder."

She said, "I want more."

I said, "Clear your breathing and say it louder."

She did.

I said, "Close your eyes and picture your husband and say the words to him." I asked her to notice what happened to her breathing as she pictured him. She did.

In the next thirty to forty minutes of our forty-five minute session, Ruth gave continued expression to her natural self, and I think she relearned some things about responsibility, choice, feelings as energy, where she ends and other folks begin, asking for what she wants, working through conflict, simply noticing, accenting the obvious, breathing, asking for help, and that she was not her mother. She left feeling a little freer and happier, and we agreed to meet again.

Ruth was the first of many clients I met with that day. I imagine they all benefited. Not because I offered profound bits of wisdom like "say it again" but because of their guts and their willingness to dive into a full-bodied experience of themselves in the Here and Now toward the goal of increased pleasure. I think that my Intention to Connect with Respect for the sacredness of the opportunity helped Ruth express herself Authentically. I trusted the process. She trusted me. And we had a good Experience.

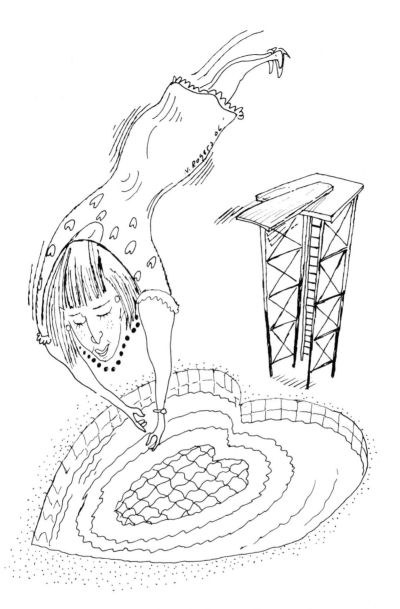

When I'm not in touch with the true love within me, the results of my work are okay, I suppose, but my feeling is more that of being a skilled robot than of being a feeling, loving, vibrant participant in life. When I'm so caught up in the task at hand that I lose touch with the love within me, my sessions become less stimulating and I think I am less effective.

I have the choice to be and do with love, or to be and do as a robot. So do you. Experiencing the love within you takes consciousness, intention, and—I won't kid you—self-discipline. It takes effort. But you can do it, and the payoff is immediate and glorious.

Allowing the love within you to manifest in actions aimed at helping others will fulfill you. You can do helpful actions in whatever arena you choose. You can do helpful actions simply by being sensitive to others, being true to yourself, and being in touch with the love that is the essence of the Natural You.

Chapter 25

So Let's Review

We've covered a lot of territory. Here is a review of at least some of what you've learned.

It's an exam in a way, the mere mention of which can bring up a barrage of gremlin chatter. (But hey, this is, after all, a Master Class.) Whether you pranced through your school days as a whiz-kid or slogged through the way I did (I managed to cram four years of undergraduate school into five), the mere mention of a test can get your gremlin snickering and plotting. If so, you know precisely what to do:

Simply Notice

Play with Options

Be in Process

1. Your _ _ _ _ is a giant warehouse filled with remnants and representations of direct experience.

2. In the warehouse, there dwells the monster of the mind—

179

your _ _ _ _ _ _ _.

3. Your _ _ _ _ _ is the home and the source of true love.

4. To help restore your emotional equilibrium after a shake-up, you might want to ask yourself four key questions: What's so? _ _ _ _ _ _ _? _ _ _ _ _ _ _? And _ _ _ _ now?

5. The Zen Theory of Change is this: I _ _ _ _ myself not by _ _ _ _ _ _ to _ _ _ _ myself, but by simply _ _ _ _ _ _ _ _ how I am _ _ _ _ _ _ _ _ _ _ _ myself in the very moment I am imprisoning myself.

6. One powerful option to play with when freeing yourself from your gremlin's grip is to accent the _ _ _ _ _ _ _.

7. The first six principles of the Gremlin-Taming Method, known as the _ _ _ _ _ _ of _ _ _ _ _ _ _ _ _, constitute a means of establishing your sense of centeredness, even in the midst of upheaval.

8. The first Basic of _ _ _ _ _ _ _ _ is this: make being cen-tered and feeling good a top _ _ _ _ _ _ _ _ _.

9. The second is this: remember that doing so is primarily an _ _ _ _ _ _ _ _ _.

10. The third Basic of Pleasure is: stay aware of where you end and all else begins, the miraculous _ _ _ _ _ _ known as your _ _ _ _.

11. The fourth Basic of Pleasure is this: _ _ _ _ _ _ _, dammit, breathe.

12. The fifth Basic of Pleasure is this: relax your _ _ _ _ to keep

your _ _ _ _ _ _ _ _.

13. The sixth is this: establish the _ _ _ _ and _ _ _ as your
_ _ _ _ _ _ _ _ from which you consciously direct your
spotlight of _ _ _ _ _ _ _ _ .

14. The next three principles of gremlin-taming are called
the Art of _ _ _ _ _ _ _ _ _ _ _ _ _. This is a three-step
process for freeing yourself from your _ _ _ _ _ _ _ _ _ _ _ -
_ _ _ _ _ _ _ _ _ _ (HPCs), your outdated Habitual
Behavior Patterns (HBPs), and your gremlin's chatter.

15. The first step in the Art of _ _ _ _ _ _ _ _ _ _ _ _ _ is this:
simply _ _ _ _ _ _.

16. The second step is this: _ _ _ _ with Options.

17. The third step is this: Be in _ _ _ _ _ _ _.

18. The last seven principles of the Gremlin-Taming
Method are represented in the acronym I CREATE.
This acronym represents a system for creating rewarding

_ _ _ _ _ _ _ _ _ _ _ _ _.

19. The I in I CREATE stands for _ _ _ _ _ _ _ _ _.

20. The C in I CREATE stands for _ _ _ _ _ _ _ _ _ _.

21. The R in I CREATE stands for _ _ _ _ _ _ _.

22. The first E in I CREATE stands for _ _ _ _ _ _ _ _ _ _.

23. The A in I CREATE stands for _ _ _ _ _ _ _ _ _ _ _.

24. The T in I CREATE stands for _ _ _ _ _.

181

25. The final E in I CREATE stands for _ _ _ _ _ _ _ _ _ _.

26. Using the phrase "_ _ _ _ _ now" will serve as a helpful reminder of your ability to change an outdated belief or behavior.

27. Service and servitude are _ _ _ the same thing.

28. SNDHBL (pronounced snidabul) is a system for simply and clearly and authentically reporting your experience. The H in SNDHBL stands for _ _ _ _.

29. Your Heart is the core of the _ _ _ _ _ _ _ you.

30. Your gremlin is _ _ _ cute!

Brain freeze on any of the above? The answers are available at www.tamingyourgremlin.com. Enter the password SNDHBL (all caps).

Chapter 26

A Note to Jim

I began our time together with a vignette ending with the phrase "When you're dead, you're a dead peckerhead." It's not a lighthearted truth or a heavy-handed pronouncement. It's just the way it seems to be.

Every relationship you have, including ours, will end. There will be a last time to relate to him, her, or it. You may leave, or he, she, or it may go, but it will end. Good-byes come with the territory.

You can lose your wallet, the big game, or a loved one. It's sandpaper-rough when it's the latter. There's just no doubt about it—it's hard when someone you love dies. Take dads, for instance.

When dads die, they take with them suit coats warm to the touch, brusque voices, and daddy pride. They carry off with them into the hereafter answers to questions never asked, favorite ditties, shared stories, hard times unexplained, and victories unsung. They drift off leaving you holding a bag of lonelies and if-onlys. There's no getting around it. It's hard when someone you love dies.

A loving soul is a loving soul, whether it's housed in a predominantly hairless body with two arms and two legs, or one with four legs and fur. If you've had a loving relationship with another soul and that soul makes his or her leap to the other side, you'll have some healing to do.

If someone you love dies, mourn. Express your feelings verbally and in writing. Do so with a clear Intention to Connect with your full experience. Respect the opportunity. Review the past, but don't try to redo it.

The true love that is the essence of your Heart will heal your pain. Dive into your memories and your pain when you feel the need. Accept unexpected waves of sadness and anger, and work with them, not against them. Breathe. Open your Heart to the experience.

Reflect on the gifts you received from having spent time with your lost loved one. Decide to cherish the gifts, to use them, and to embellish them. Forgive your loved one for dying. This, too, takes time. Intend to forgive. Find the desire to let go of your loved one. Let go of him or her. Keep the good memories and wisdom you gained from your loved one's life and death.

So what is it you say good-bye to when you say good-bye to a loved one? "Essence" comes close. There literally is no word for it, so let's use that one. Each person you have ever connected with has a unique essence—a unique feel—and produces a unique experience within you. It may be similar to the experience you have of others, but it's not the same. It's unique. And when it's gone, it's gone. But you can access it through memory for moments at a time, and during these moments, you can feel your lost loved ones in your Heart.

It's not the same as hugging and holding, but that Heart can love and feel them as richly as ever.

So to Jim Turnbow I'd like to say, "When you're dead, you're not dead, you peckerhead."

Chapter 27

It's Been a Slice

We've covered everything from love to loss. My heartfelt desire is that this book has made you more conscious of the gift of your life and of your choices about how to spend it, breath to breath. Writing it has done so for me.

I've done my level best to offer advice that goes from my Heart to yours. It's all offered in the spirit of love and friendship, and I hope that for you, it strikes a chord of common experience and resonates with common sense. Mostly I hope it is a stepping-stone on the path toward finding the true love that is the essence of who you really are.

I wish you increasing pleasure in your life and appreciation of it, and I hope, too, that you will never get a tattoo. By the way, if you already have one, here's my advice: don't get another one.